A Century of Juvenile Justice

by Philip W. Harris, Wayne N. Welsh, and Frank Butler

A B S T R A C T

The millennium marks the beginning of a second century for the formal system of juvenile justice in the United States. From its inception, the central focus of the system has been delinquency, an amorphous construct that includes not only "criminal" behavior but also an array of youthful actions that offend prevailing social mores. Thus, the meaning of delinquency is markedly time dependent. Likewise, methods for addressing the phenomenon have reflected the vagaries of social constructions of youth and youth deviance. American juvenile justice was founded on internally conflicting value systems: the diminished responsibility and heightened malleability of youths versus individual culpability and social control of protocriminality. During its first century, the latter generally have become increasingly predominant over the former. Those most caught up in the system, however, have remained overwhelmingly our most marginalized youths, from immigrants' offspring in the early 20th century to children of color in contemporary society. The implications of such theoretical and sociodemographic variations are considered, and their implications are reviewed for public policy beyond mere political symbolism.

Philip W. Harris, Ph.D., and Wayne N. Welsh, Ph.D., are Associate Professors and Frank Butler, J.D., M.B.A., is an Instructor in the Department of Criminal Justice at Temple University.

From the vantage point of those living in the 21st century, perhaps one way the previous century will be recalled is as one in which the state became elaborately involved in issues of youthful deviance in the United States. From the beginning of the 20th century and all the way through to its closure, the discourse of "juvenile justice" has remained prominent, in marked contrast to prior periods.

Traditional societal concern with the need for instilling law-abiding attitudes and behaviors in its young took on new prominence in the 20th century, as elaborate processes were put into place to promote conformity. Government— personified in a special judiciary—was at the helm and remained preeminent as the new juvenile justice "system" voyaged through the uncharted waters of changing social constructions of youth deviance. For most of this time, the seas have remained turbulent, due in large part to inherently contradictory aims of the enterprise: to protect youths and support those in trouble and also to punish youths and protect society from them.

In spite of this basic inconsistency, the juvenile system has been impelled consistently by powerful rhetoric about youths, a rhetoric that is largely mythic but highly politicized. For example, at the beginning of the century, the Progressive agenda of segregating and salvaging youths who defied social mores was underlain, at least in part, by the popular eugenicist goal of discouraging reproduction among the dangerous classes (Haller [1963] 1984). Toward the end of the century, beginning in the late 1970s, responses to juvenile crime toughened much more than can be explained by juvenile involvement in crime. During this period, people over 18 years of age committed a much greater proportion of all crime than juveniles; property crime rates remained much higher than violent crime rates and essentially unchanged; and juveniles continued to comprise small proportions of all arrests. However, vindictive approaches to youth crime reached new peaks during this period. For the most part, public policy has not been strongly related to patterns in delinquency.

One particularly troubling aspect of juvenile justice as it has been constructed throughout the 20th century is its disproportionate involvement, in an aggregate social sense, with youths from the lowest socioeconomic strata, who at least in the latter half of the 20th century overwhelmingly have been children of color. This presents special hazards in eras (such as the "crime control" period that began in about 1980) in which the punitive engines of the system overtake the more reformative ones (such as existed in the era of "juvenile rights" in roughly the 1960s and 1970s).

This chapter examines multiple forces that have substantially impacted the juvenile justice endeavor during the 20th century. An examination of shifts in policy and practice over time provides a valuable foundation for envisioning justice for youths in the new century. First, we describe the development of the juvenile justice system, underscoring major eras in its evolution. We then examine trends in four broad areas that have shaped the juvenile justice system: (1) social constructions of childhood and delinquency; (2) the role of criminological theory and measurement; (3) juvenile crime patterns as represented primarily in official reports; and (4) general social, economic, and cultural trends, including patterns of change in the larger criminal justice system. Finally, we examine the possibilities for at least ameliorating some of the seemingly intractable dilemmas of justice for youths.

Creating and Reengineering Juvenile Justice

In the 19th century, a collaboration between the demands of the Industrial Revolution, already operating at full steam, and the sentiments of religious reformers, who sought outlets for their need to save the downtrodden, led to organized efforts to discipline deviant youths deemed not beyond the pale of reformation (Fox 1970). Institutionalization with fellow youthful deviants was viewed as the principal, beneficent intervention needed to inculcate middle-class, Protestant, rural values and ethics among the hordes of immigrant offspring in urban slums. Houses of refuge established to serve the poor evolved into places of incarceration. The prevalent moral view was that pauperism and nascent criminality were mutually reinforcing, such that removal from the family of origin was the preferred pathway to moral regeneration for children of the "dangerous classes."

Efforts to save wayward youths from the corrupting effects of poverty and vice became increasingly organized, culminating in the institution of juvenile courts, the first of which was established in Illinois in 1899. The majesty of the law could now be used formally to further the efforts of primarily religious agencies to instill nondeviant norms in children who acted—or appeared likely to act—in ways disdained by the majority culture. The normalizing philosophy, which in the early 20th century justified the creation of juvenile courts, contributed heavily to a perspective that has endured in juvenile court jurisprudence: the "best interest" of lower class children entails coercion into middle-class values rather than any sort of serious consideration of more profound issues of distributive or social justice.

In its inception, the juvenile court was not a radical break with past practice. In Illinois, for example, the creation of the court was widely supported by dominant elites (Platt 1977). Vested penological interests, including reform schools

The punitive aspects of the court were hidden under the rubric of enlightened, well-intentioned reform of the child, and criminal trappings were simply defined away through euphemism, e.g., the legal fiction that juvenile court proceedings were civil rather than criminal matters.

and industrial schools, were positioned to profit from the court's jurisdiction, and to this day a wide array of agencies of social control are wholly dependent on the juvenile court's propensity to intrude liberally into the lives of its charges. Despite rhetoric regarding the value of home and family, the court's founders were happy to invoke correctional cures for lower class youths whose families permitted them to engage in behavior judged to be immoral by conventional standards: "drinking, begging, roaming the streets, frequenting dance-halls and movies, fighting, sexuality, staying out late at night, and incorrigibility" (Platt 1977, 139).

With the accession in the early 20th century of "scientific" methods (mainly psychiatry and social work) of exploring human behavior, coupled with social Darwinism and the popularization of positivist criminology, the original religious underpinnings for the juvenile system waned. Positivists confidently identified traits and conditions that were precursors to adult criminality, developing "treatment" modalities to cure these pathologies among hapless youths. The state as parent, personified in the juvenile court judge, was privileged to exercise solicitude, as well as mete out discipline, by committing increasing numbers of children to the care of professional reformers. The work of the juvenile court was perceived to be in the best interest not only of the child but of everyone (Rothman 1980).

Ironically, in its origins the juvenile court was designed as an appendage to the new social welfare professions. In contrast to the procedural, legal ceremony endemic to adult courts, the juvenile court was to be characterized by mere "ceremonial legality" (Sutton 1985). In its superficial informality, it symbolically projected a nonlegal, solicitous posture toward its youthful clientele. A major theoretical justification for the court's nonlegal or extralegal *modus operandi* was the doctrine of *parens patriae*, traditionally invoked by English chancery courts to prevent waste of property subject to ownership by minors and incompetents. Although chancery did not use *parens patriae* as a basis for any sort of prosecutorial proceedings, American juvenile courts liberally cited it as their jurisprudential foundation, disguising the actual precedents for their activities, namely, police power and the Elizabethan Poor Laws intended to control pauper children (Wizner 1995).

It made little or no difference whether a child was deemed delinquent or merely dependent/neglected. Both were in need of moral cure, and both would profit from the same scientifically approved methods of treatment in the same institutions. In delinquency, the concern was not primarily with the charges but rather with a youth's character, background, and psychological makeup. Essentially, not their acts but their souls were at issue. The discretionary power of the healers to determine the cure and the length of treatment for its effectiveness rendered legal formality pointless. The punitive aspects of the court were hidden under the rubric of enlightened, well-intentioned reform of the child, and criminal trappings were simply defined away through euphemism, e.g., the legal fiction that juvenile court proceedings were civil rather than criminal matters.

Jurisdiction over "status" offenses—an amorphous class of behaviors that were viewed as indicators of future delinquency—provided a rich source of clients for the courts' paternalistic oversight. Although similar behaviors were widely ignored by the legal system when they were exhibited by adults, juvenile courts saw their role as enforcing the dependence of childhood in the face of threats of premature adulthood (Rothman 1980).

The predominant informality of the juvenile courts facilitated wide discretion for juvenile court judges, both in adjudication and disposition. Additionally, deliberately vague statutory definitions of delinquency and dependency allowed the courts to intervene, quite arbitrarily, in an exceptionally broad array of family issues, particularly when the families were of the lower classes and implicitly in need of humanitarian corrective services.

Gradually, and probably heavily influenced by the widespread impoverishment of even the morally upright during the Great Depression, the optimistic outlook that crime reduction could be achieved by treating symptomatic lower class children became suspect (Fox 1970). The juvenile system became recognized increasingly as a mechanism for social control of nascent criminality. Disenchantment with the rehabilitative ideal became apparent as juvenile institutions adopted more emphasis on incapacitation and deterrent technologies. Eventually, the design of the system emerged from the shadows of the *parens patriae* mythology, offending the expansive social conscience that characterized the 1960s.

Legalism as an elixir

Candid condemnation of even the juvenile court, the apex of the juvenile system, was undertaken by no less an authority than the U.S. Supreme Court. Demanding "domestication" of the "kangaroo" juvenile court, the Court premised the possibility of redemption on the incorporation of procedural due process (*In re Gault*,

The late 1970s through the 1990s have witnessed simultaneous, substantial growth in both incarcerative and diversionary approaches to troublesome youths.

387 U.S. 1 [1967]). Notice of charges, the right to counsel, the right to confrontation/cross-examination, and the right against compelled self-incrimination were all formally incorporated into the juvenile court as part of the "due process" revolution of the late 1960s. The Court declined, however, to mandate a constitutional right to jury trial in the juvenile court, fearing that such a step would signal the beginning of the end for juvenile courts (*McKeiver* v. *Pennsylvania*, 403 U.S. 528 [1971]).

Finally, consistent with the more punitive Zeitgeist of the 1980s, the Court rejected sociological data about the futility of predicting future dangerousness and instead held that pretrial detention of juveniles based on "serious risk" does not violate the principle of fundamental fairness required by due process (*Schall* v. *Martin*, 467 U.S. 253 [1984]). In fact, the Court, by its observation that adolescents were never fully free of adult supervision, reaffirmed the image that adolescence is a subcategory of childhood.

Particularly since the 1980s, the focus of juvenile courts has been on the offense committed (what has been termed the "principle of offense") rather than on the treatment of the juvenile (Feld 1988). So-called legal considerations (mainly the relative severity of a given offense, coupled with the accused's official record of past offenses) trump concerns about a youth's future well-being. Indeed, the essence of the modern juvenile court hearing has been described as "little substance, much legal ritual, all flow control" (Humes 1996). Because the original raison d'être for the juvenile court was rooted in individualized rehabilitation, the increased exposure of standardized, punitive dimensions of the court has raised the possibility of simplification by merging juvenile courts with adult criminal courts.

Procedural protections afforded in juvenile court, insofar as they exist, have not necessarily been salutary for juveniles. The adversarial model is now publicly recognized as the core of the juvenile system, yet at least one major study has found that unrepresented juveniles receive less severe dispositions than their counterparts who are represented, even when controlling for relative severity of offense, pretrial detention status, and prior official records (Feld 1993b). Additionally, in spite of the lip service paid to legal representation, substantial proportions of juveniles are unrepresented, and this has not impeded the popularity of "repeat offender" dispositions based partly or wholly on uncounseled prior convictions (Feld 1989).

Considering the community as part of the cure

Although the dominant theme in youth corrections through at least the first half of the 20th century was institution based, the general disaffection for social institutions during the 1960s contributed to approaches based in prevention, diversion, and deinstitutionalization (Miller 1991). Massive Federal funding from the new Law Enforcement Assistance Administration in the 1970s encouraged a proliferation of programs designed to spare redeemable youths the formality and stigma of the juvenile court. The 1974 Juvenile Justice and Delinquency Prevention Act placed great emphasis on community-based treatment, and it included a prohibition against incarcerating status offenders in secure detention and correctional facilities. Deinstitutionalization became fashionable, though it was reserved largely for status offenders. Nonincarcerative settings included group homes, nonresidential therapeutic communities, day treatment centers, and wilderness programs. Evaluations of such programs, however, have failed to demonstrate appreciable reductions in youth deviance (Welsh, Harris, and Jenkins 1996).

The late 1970s through the 1990s have witnessed simultaneous, substantial growth in both incarcerative and diversionary approaches to troublesome youths. At least two meta-analyses have been undertaken. In a study of 90 community-based programs, it was found that the most effective were those that were most intense, most closely monitored for implementation problems, most community oriented, and most focused on developing specific life skills (Gottschalk et al. 1987). Another study of 44 juvenile and 23 adult treatment programs concluded that effectiveness depended largely on delivering appropriate services to higher risk individuals, targeting criminogenic needs, and matching intervention with client needs and learning styles. What the authors deemed inappropriate services increased subsequent deviance if they were delivered in the residential rather than community setting (Andrews et al. 1990).

The proliferation of the treatment industry that is an appendage of the juvenile court has also included specialized programs that increasingly are based on medical models. For example, specialized programs for youthful drug offenders and sex offenders purport to reduce such antisocial tendencies. The full panoply of the health care industry—from accreditation through the Joint Commission on Accreditation of Healthcare Organizations to insurance arrangements through managed care—is finding untapped markets in youthful deviance. Privatization of services is becoming increasingly common in areas such as drug treatment, foster care, and education as for-profit corporations realize the lucrative potential in youth corrections on which they have already capitalized in adult corrections.

This evolving coexistence of contradictory goals, such as treatment and punishment, is exemplified by the National Juvenile Justice Action Plan, part of the Office of Juvenile Justice and Delinquency Prevention's (OJJDP's)

Comprehensive Strategy for Serious, Violent, and Chronic Juvenile Offenders (Wilson and Howell 1993). One objective of this plan is to provide immediate intervention and appropriate sanctions and treatment for delinquents. The SafeFutures project funded under this objective seeks collaboration among juvenile authorities, health and mental health providers, educators, and neighborhood boards. A second objective is the prosecution of serious, violent, and chronic juvenile defendants in criminal court. For example, OJJDP funds research on waiver mechanisms. A third objective, the reduction of youth involvement with guns, drugs, and gangs, invokes the stereotypical trilogy of urban youths. Funding under this objective includes the Boston Violence Prevention Project, the National Youth Gang Suppression and Intervention Program, the Comprehensive Response to America's Youth Gang Initiative, the National Youth Gang Center, and the Boys & Girls Clubs of America's Gang Prevention through Targeted Outreach. A fourth objective involves providing educational and mentoring opportunities for youths considered at risk. Included here are programs such as the Violence Prevention Curriculum for Adolescents, the Program for Youth Negotiators, peer mediation programs, Positive Action Through Holistic Education (PATHE), and Juvenile Mentoring Programs (JUMP). Finally, a fifth objective is to address youth victimization, abuse, and neglect, for which OJJDP funds programs such as Safe Kids/Safe Streets (family service agencies), the Healthy Start program (comprehensive child health services in infancy and early childhood), and the Yale/New Haven Child Development–Community Policing Program.

This brief discussion of juvenile justice history suggests four eras that can be distinguished by dominant policy themes: (1) the Refuge Period (1824–98), (2) the Juvenile Court Period (1899–1960), (3) the Juvenile Rights Period (1961–80), and (4) the Crime Control Period (1981–present). The latter era is evolving into a more complex policy period as Federal, State, and local authorities attempt to reconcile divergent policy paths. As we discuss the broader set of forces that have helped to shape the juvenile justice system, we will link trends in these forces to these periods.

The Social Constructions of Childhood and Delinquency

Underlying the development of the juvenile justice system are disturbing images of children as victims and children as offenders. These images are structured in terms of two evolving social constructs that directly influence social responses to juvenile delinquency: the meaning of childhood and the meaning of delinquency. The meaning of delinquency, of course, is to a great extent a consequence of how society defines childhood. Even today, the legal and psychological communities grapple with the relationship between theories of child development and the boundary separating criminal from delinquent, seeking ways to shield young people from unfair treatment by the justice system and resolve bothersome contradictions in youth policy.

In the past few years, the United States has experienced an explosion of punitiveness directed at its young. Between 1983 and 1995, the percentage of juveniles held in public facilities increased by 47 percent (Sickmund 1997). Moreover, at the end of this period, nearly every State revised its juvenile justice legislation, increasing the range of offenses eligible for juvenile court exclusion, reducing the confidentiality of juvenile court proceedings and records, and more clearly linking sanctions to offenses (Szymanski 1997; Torbet et al. 1996). These changes, since they occurred so rapidly across the Nation, suggest a new image of the juvenile delinquent, but one that has yet to be articulated.

The meaning of childhood

Our concepts of childhood and adolescence have developed since the inception of the juvenile court, as has knowledge regarding child and adolescent development. Earlier images of the child as innocent and in need of adult protection have given way to views that are more complex and that have resulted in social contexts that are both more permissive and more demanding. Today's children have access to information previously regarded as harmful, and they command a significant share of the marketplace. The children's rights movement and tentative parenting of the 1970s, or the Juvenile Rights Period, have been replaced by a theme of individual accountability in the 1990s (Bazemore 1992; Torbet et al. 1996). Simultaneously, expectations of parents, children, and adults generally occupy a more prominent place in policy discussions regarding delinquency and adolescent substance abuse. Parents, teachers, and even adult neighbors are being encouraged to exercise more control over our young.

Scholars who have examined the history of juvenile justice agree that childhood is "better seen as a social fact than a biological one" (Ainsworth 1999, 8; see also Empey 1978; Aries 1962). Childhood is an invention. The practice of carving up human maturation into distinct stages, and then attaching to different stages different amounts of cultural capital, extends well beyond the science of human biology. Aries' (1962) historical account of childhood informs us of the apparent lack of distinction between child and adult in medieval society. No effort was made to protect children from the social life of adults; no perceived reason for protection had yet emerged. The notion of the innocence of children would come later.

Ainsworth (1999) notes the contradiction between Calvinist doctrine of being born into sin and thus doomed to eternal damnation and the philosophy of the Enlightenment that saw children as pure and innocent and thus in need of protection and nurturing. The former view suggests the need for salvation, whereas the latter implies the need to avoid noxious, criminogenic influences in the environment until the immunization brought on by proper socialization can withstand the forces of evil. Underlying both of these images of childhood was the notion that children are different from adults and that adults play a role in shaping who they become. The contest between these two views was played out in the facilities known as Houses of Refuge that proliferated under the watchful eyes of sectarian organizations during the 19th century. Although primarily intended to serve the poor, their roles as child care enterprises evolved as interest in the deleterious effects of burgeoning urban areas grew (Empey 1978).

Around the time of the creation of the juvenile court, the structuring of childhood continued with renewed vigor. The "child study" movement not only produced more complex descriptions of stages of development, but became formalized as universities established departments of child development and as medicine developed its field of pediatrics (Ainsworth 1999).

Important for juvenile justice, the developmental stage of adolescence emerged as a means of describing persons who are developmentally between childhood and adulthood. Marking this boundary became the focus of policy development, most vividly expressed in child labor laws and compulsory school attendance laws. Preoccupation with controlling persons perceived to be a threat to the social order, by virtue of their physical size and lack of maturity, resulted in the stretching of the length of childhood and the consequent economic dependency of teenagers, creating even greater demands for formal social control. From a justice system perspective, society elected to classify adolescents as a subclass of children, as opposed to adults, and thus chose to not hold teenagers accountable for their behavior. As stated by Ainsworth (1999, 12), "to the advocates of the juvenile court, the essential difference between the moral and cognitive capacities of the juvenile and those of the adult did not serve merely to mitigate juvenile culpability for breaking the law, but also to absolve the juvenile completely from criminal liability." Once committed to a strategy of control over this vibrant segment of society, control became an obsession. The juvenile court, with its doctrine of *parens patriae*, became the ultimate tool of control. Without the constraints of due process, the juvenile court judge was free to prescribe forms of "treatment" that would bring about changes in behavior and lifestyle. Social construction is ultimately a utilitarian enterprise. By the mid 1960s, the image of adolescence that had animated the juvenile court since its creation had been rendered impotent. The shift from a rehabilitative ideology to one based on retribution did not occur in response to changes in our beliefs about the causes of delinquent behavior; rather, this change occurred in response to a general disillusionment with our capacity to rehabilitate and our fear of the potential harm brought about by the actions of teenagers. Policymakers chose to give up on *parens patriae*, on seeing adolescence as a subset of childhood, because the strategy of treatment failed to control the behavior of unruly teenagers. Gradually, adolescence was reclassified as a subset of adulthood, and retributive principles were again viewed as appropriate in assigning sanctions in juvenile cases.

> *The violent juvenile has been a regular news feature for more than a decade. Although the problems of guns and violence require attention, they distract the public from the fact that violent youths are not the norm.*

Legislative bodies have not been alone in the reconstruction of adolescence; the courts have tackled several critical questions pertaining to the rights and responsibilities of children and parents. The Supreme Court decisions of the 1960s implied that children were persons deserving of the same constitutional protections available to adults, including free speech, due process rights, and making important decisions (Gardner 1995). Other decisions reinforce the authority of parents and school administrators, including mature minor provisions regarding the requirement of parental consent to receive nonemergency medical care, especially birth control, abortion, and substance abuse treatment. Inconsistencies among these decisions regarding the autonomy of adolescents underscore the ambivalence of policymakers about the nature of adolescence itself.

The form of punishment adopted during the latter part of the Crime Control Period (1980 to the present) has been a modified version of that found in the criminal courts. We say modified, because competency development, a component of the "balanced approach" that has replaced the rehabilitation mission of many juvenile court statutes, has been incorporated as an aim of most recently adopted juvenile court acts (Bazemore 1992). The balanced approach comprises consideration for public safety, offender accountability, and competency development of the offender, with public safety being an overriding concern. More weight is now given to the needs of the victim in crafting sanctions, and, in practice, restitution has received renewed emphasis. Competency development, according to this schema, has to do with increasing the ability of the offender to play socially acceptable roles through education, vocational training, and improvements in social skills. A lack of competence, however, is not a defense against accountability.

In contrast to this emphasis on accountability are recent reactions to the school shootings in Littleton, Colorado, and elsewhere. Discussions among legislators and citizens reported by the media suggest that communities are rethinking the amount of autonomy that should be extended to adolescents. This instability of the social construct of adolescence mirrors the ambivalence that adults have regarding the application of informal mechanisms of social control to youths who are nearing adulthood.

Recent literature on adolescence suggests that moral panic characterizes adult reactions to every new generation of adolescent (Bernard 1992; Brendtro and Long 1994; Moore and Tonry 1998; Austin and Willard 1998). According to Austin and Willard (1998, 1):

> "Youth" becomes a metaphor for perceived social change and its projected consequences, and as such it is an enduring locus for displaced social anxieties. Pronouncements such as "the problems of youth today," used as a scapegoat for larger social concerns, objectify and reify young people *as the problem in itself.* (emphasis in original)

The images that are shaping juvenile justice are even more threatening. Gangs, some of them national in scope; drug trafficking; drive-by shootings; and guns have been linked, often in ways that are unsupported by research findings, to support the image of the superpredator (DiIulio 1996). Although DiIulio has been criticized for promoting this view of the juvenile delinquent (see, e.g., Howell 1997, 195), such images are not new. The violent juvenile has been a regular news feature for more than a decade. Although the problems of guns and violence require attention, they distract the public from the fact that violent youths are not the norm. The business of juvenile justice is more about young people who are like delinquents have always been and the families, schools and neighborhoods that shape their lives.

Definitions of delinquency interweave criminal behavior and individual characteristics. That is, the status of delinquent has traditionally been attributed to individuals on the basis of life conditions, the offense being less significant than the larger set of circumstances.

The meaning of delinquency

The early years of the juvenile justice system relied heavily on the Christian metaphor of salvation (Platt 1977). Children of the poor were viewed as being raised in home and neighborhood environments in which proper parenting was absent, parents were uncaring, homes were unfit for raising children, and neighborhoods were hotbeds of immorality and vice

(Schlossman and Sedlak 1983). Since delinquency has traditionally meant more than criminal behavior, and because the salvation metaphor fell to the influence of science, more recent discussions of prevention and treatment have relied on medical analogies and metaphors of science, implying that delinquency was some sort of illness (Asquith 1983). With salvation and rehabilitation serving as philosophical options, the juvenile justice system was not designed to consider conduct alone as the proper subject of its decisions.

Beginning in the 1960s—the Juvenile Rights Period—developments in the sociology of deviance shifted the focus of criminology away from the causes of delinquency to the machinery of justice and the actions of its agents. Labeling theory and research on discretion led many criminologists and policymakers to conclude that the search for causes of delinquency was futile. Moreover, deviance theorists argued that the real purpose of the juvenile justice system might have more to do with the ideological views and political dynamics of these systems of social control than with their stated noble aims.

The fact that the juvenile court process derived from criminal justice and has come to resemble criminal court processing presents the juvenile justice system with a problem. The court process must view the individual offender as a rational, responsible person, but the correctional process assumes pathology or lack of socialization (Duster 1987). During the 1970s, when rehabilitation suffered its greatest defeats, juvenile correctional programs remained faithful to their rehabilitative aims. All of the actions against rehabilitation occurred within the context of the court; corrections remained largely untouched by the changes that were taking place in the larger arena of juvenile justice. The tension between these perspectives reflects the ambivalence of our culture with regard to its adolescents. Their unequal status in comparison to adults is well established, but adult authority structures have been reluctant to assume responsibility for their behavior (Empey and Stafford 1991).

Definitions of delinquency interweave criminal behavior and individual characteristics. That is, the status of delinquent has traditionally been attributed to individuals on the basis of life conditions, the offense being less significant than the larger set of circumstances. During the Crime Control Period, with juvenile offending regarded as a serious threat to public safety, the court became more offense focused, both in terms of evaluating cases and in terms of imposing sanctions. Graduated sanctions are now accepted as proper within the juvenile court, where once the offense played a relatively minor role. Additionally, the expanded use of waivers emphasizes the importance of the offense in judging the appropriateness of a youth for delinquency programs. This trend has been supported by an explosion of legislation and by recent case law that have articulated an end to rehabilitation as the central aim of juvenile justice.

Status offenses, which were largely ignored in recent years, have now become causes for referral to prevention and diversion programs and tools for maintaining social boundaries (Krisberg and Austin 1993). Distinguishing status offenses from delinquent offenses became a critical policy issue in the 1970s, largely due to attacks on the unfairness of sanctioning both categories of behavior as if they were equal. The recent revival of interest in status offenses during the Crime Control Period suggests that the traditional role of the juvenile justice system, although not necessarily involving the court, continues to have merit. That is, although status offenses continue to be seen as less serious than delinquent offenses, ensuring that children attend school, respond appropriately to parental authority, and reside at home can prevent delinquent behavior. This policy trend suggests that communities are beginning to increase the exercise of adult authority over the lives of young people.

The Role of Theory and Measurement

The social construction of delinquency has, to some degree, been influenced by the contributions of modern criminology. In other words, scientific methods have had some bearing on how we think about delinquency and respond to it. However, as we argue throughout this chapter, major shifts in juvenile justice policy only occasionally correspond to observable patterns in delinquency or new developments in theory. It would be a grand illusion to suggest that delinquency theory and measurement are the only, or even major, determinants of juvenile justice policy.

At the same time, however, methods of delinquency measurement and attention to statistical data have gradually assumed greater prominence both in delinquency theory development and juvenile justice policymaking. Delinquency theorists and juvenile justice policymakers simply do not pay attention to the same information at the same time with the same emphases.

The study of delinquency gained momentum during the Refuge Period (1824–98) with a shift toward *positivism* in science (i.e., an emphasis on observable, measurable events and behavior; an attempt to discover causal relationships assumed to exist in nature). Positivism was a reaction to earlier "classical" criminology that emphasized human rationality and the need to encourage people to responsibly exercise their free will. Although delinquency-specific theory during this period is scarce, juvenile justice advocates at that time were focused on providing large numbers of homeless and neglected delinquents with shelter, food, and discipline and teaching good work and study habits. The negative effects of the environment, they believed, could potentially be ameliorated through intervention.

Positivist criminologists began to increasingly argue three points: (1) delinquency was strongly influenced by physical, mental, and social factors; (2)
delinquents were different from nondelinquents; and (3) science could be used
profitably to discover the causes of delinquency and reduce it (Vold, Bernard,
and Snipes 1998). Two implications of this emerging perspective were that any
theory of delinquency should be based on measurable, observable behavior and
that any intervention, including punishment, should be tailored to the individual
needs of the offender. Major shifts in juvenile justice over time can be linked to
this ongoing tension between positivist and classical principles.

Much delinquency research during the Juvenile Court Period (1899–1961) (e.g.,
Glueck and Glueck 1950; Shaw and McKay 1942) struggled to uncover major,
observable, generalizable patterns in delinquent behavior. This is not to say that
such work was atheoretical, but ". . . their essential contribution was a set of
hard-won, reliable facts necessary to a scientific criminology" (Gottfredson and
Hirschi 1987, 19).[1] The Juvenile Court Period was also characterized by several
influential theoretical contributions derived largely from major sociological and
philosophical perspectives. These included Cohen's (1955) *Delinquent Boys* and
Cloward and Ohlin's (1960) *Delinquency and Opportunity*.

During this period, positivist criminologists championed the ability of scientists
to discover and change the biological, psychological, and social correlates of
delinquency. The medical model dominated thinking about crime and delinquency for much of this period, including belief in the possibility of prevention
and cure (rehabilitation).

The most sophisticated early attempts to measure and understand delinquency
grew out of the "Chicago School" research of the 1920s (e.g., Park, Burgess, and
McKenzie [1925] 1967; McKenzie 1925). Such studies, as James Short (1998, 6)
notes, were groundbreaking in their rich descriptions of delinquent lives,
including but not limited to juvenile involvement in criminal activities: " [T]he
Chicago School developed a sensitivity to process—ecological processes, organizational and institutional processes, processes of identity formation and group
processes—processes by which we become human and function as human
beings." Whereas earlier ecological research (e.g., Thrasher 1927) undertook
detailed qualitative research, including participant observation of delinquent
gangs, later research (e.g., Shaw and McKay 1942) relied increasingly on official
statistics (e.g., arrest rates and dispositions) to measure and study delinquency.

Shaw and McKay developed quantitative measures to test the social disorganization theory developed by Burgess ([1925] 1967) and others. Their theory
had two main components. First, people compete for desirable space in a city.
There was an economic advantage associated with being near the marketplace,

and most cities grew around the marketplace. Second, levels of social organization and integration varied in different communities, with corresponding effects on the socialization and behavior of youths.

They found that crime rates were highest near the center of the city and tended to decrease as one moved outward. Their explanation centered on changes in the physical environment and resultant impacts on the social behavior of residents. As the central city became too crowded and too expensive, stable businesses and residents moved out. The resulting area around the central city became a zone in transition, characterized by high mobility, social disorganization, and high rates of delinquency. They were struck by the stability of crime rates in particular communities over time, even after considerable population turnover. More recent ecological research has focused on measuring social cohesion and disorganization in different communities, as well as on other variables hypothesized to mediate the effects of community characteristics (e.g., high rates of poverty and mobility) on crime rates (e.g., Bursik 1988; Bursik and Grasmick 1993; Sampson and Lauritsen 1993; Sampson, Raudenbush and Earls 1997).

Shaw and McKay believed that a major contribution of their work was the demonstration that observed relationships between community racial composition and delinquency rates had more to do with *social structure and change* than individual motivation. Arguments by the original ecologists focused on the competition for desirable resources, including land (McKenzie 1925). Segregation was a result of competition among different groups, with European immigrants who had been in the city the longest competing most favorably. The African-American economic experience was unique because of persistent discrimination in spite of post-Civil War emancipation and reconstruction.

Few works have had greater influence on delinquency research and theory than Shaw and McKay's (Bursik 1988). As Gibbons (1979, 44) puts it, "Shaw and McKay's findings were incorporated into the background assumptions on which various sociological theories of crime and delinquency were subsequently constructed." For example, social disorganization theory was the macrolevel precursor to Hirschi's (1969) individual-level control theory (Messner and Rosenfeld 1997). Finestone (1976, 1977) illustrates how virtually all theoretical and empirical work in the field of criminology since 1929, including subcultural theories, learning theories (e.g., differential association), labeling theories, and social process theories, can be traced as extensions of or reactions to the research conducted by Shaw and McKay.

In the early part of the Juvenile Rights Period (1961–80), the importance of social and cultural influences on delinquency gained prominence for a time, largely as a result of the emergence and appeal of Cloward and Ohlin's (1960) differential opportunity theory and accompanying social interventions under the Johnson presidency such as the war on poverty and the Great Society (e.g., education, job training, skills training, community resource centers). Like the earlier human ecologists, Cloward and Ohlin argued that individual motivations did not by themselves explain delinquency. Instead, the individual must be in a deviant or conforming environment that allows him or her to learn requisite skills and abilities. The deprivation of legitimate means produces a strain toward delinquency, but behavioral adaptations can take many different forms, depending on exactly what specific illegitimate opportunities are available in the environment. Legitimate opportunities may be blocked, but illegitimate ones must be available before the individual can choose one or the other. If delinquency emerges because of unequal opportunity and the widespread availability of illegitimate opportunities, then the clear policy implications of this theory are that alternatives to delinquent subcultures and illegitimate opportunities must be provided.

Labeling theory also garnered attention during the 1960s and 1970s, leading to policy emphases on prevention, diversion, and even deinstitutionalization. Labeling theory focuses on the informal and formal application of stigmatizing labels by various persons on those who misbehave. Secondary deviance emerges when one engages in additional deviant behavior attributable to stigmatization and changes in self-concept rather than the original deviant behavior. The perspective caught on, leading to a widely shared assumption that established systems of control produced more crime than they prevented (Empey 1978). The juvenile diversion movement of the 1970s was in large part attributable to the influence of labeling theory.

Labeling theory has at least partly guided more current theories, including Braithwaite's (1989) concept of reintegrative shaming. Reintegrative shaming describes processes by which a deviant is labeled and sanctioned but brought back into the community of law-abiding citizens through various words, gestures, or rituals. The stigmatization or "deviance amplification" process, in contrast, occurs only when no attempt is made to reconcile offenders with their communities. This perspective incorporates variables from various other theories (e.g., control theory and social learning theory), though, and certainly cannot be categorized as a recycled version of labeling theory.

Compatible with labeling theory is the view that most delinquent behavior occurs within the context of normal adolescent development. Even very high-rate offenders (a small fraction of all delinquents) do not engage in delinquent behavior all the time. The great majority of juveniles are engaged in normal, law-abiding behaviors most of the time (Matza 1964). Many juveniles "drift" into occasional delinquency when social controls are weakened (Matza and Sykes 1961; Sykes and Matza 1957), but most age out of delinquency entirely as they approach adulthood.

The popularity of theories that shifted responsibility from individuals to criminogenic environments was partly attributable to widely held views of the time that agents of social control were often unfair, negligent, or even brutal. By the early 1980s, the pendulum had shifted toward more conservative crime-control policies, and interest in opportunity and labeling theories faded (see the concluding section of this chapter).

Sophistication in measuring delinquency has improved greatly since 1960, and delinquency studies have become increasingly informed by the empirical measurement and observation of behavior. Although all measures still retain certain limitations, we are, in general, able to better control for measurement error through developments in statistical and analytical techniques as well as large probability samples. Ideally, many believed,[2] ongoing advances in the measurement of delinquency would advance the development of both useful theories and effective policies. Positivist ideals strongly influenced delinquency theory and policy development during the Juvenile Rights Period.

Four broad types of public institutions collect delinquency data (Reiss and Roth 1993, 37): (1) the criminal justice system, (2) the juvenile justice system, (3) social services (e.g., mental health, alcohol and drug abuse, physical and sexual abuse), and (4) the public health system (e.g., injuries and deaths due to different causes). The first two are used most often to study delinquency patterns and causes.

Since the appearance of Short and Nye's (1958) groundbreaking study, self-report data have increasingly been used to study delinquency (Farrington 1973; Farrington et al. 1996; Hindelang, Hirschi, and Weis 1981; Huizinga and Elliott 1986). Self-report measures of delinquency became particularly popular in the 1960s, exemplified by Hirschi's (1969) conceptualization of control theory and its accompanying self-report scales. Further development of individually oriented theories (e.g., social learning theories) led to exponential growth of delinquency self-report measures.

Although considerable variation in delinquency is reported depending on items used (e.g., type and seriousness of behaviors), sampling strategies, and technique (e.g., survey versus interview), self-report delinquency measures offer several advantages. Self-report measures, like victimization measures, can detect crimes that were not reported to police. Most important, self-report measures can ask various causal questions related to individual motivations for committing a crime, including questions about attitudes, peer associations, family structure and relationships, and socioeconomic status. Although greater attention to reliability and validity issues is still needed, self-reported delinquency measures have often demonstrated good concurrent and predictive validity in relation to criteria such as juvenile court petitions (Farrington et al. 1996; Huizinga and Elliott 1986).

Although the tension between classical and positivistic criminology has never completely abated, and the hegemony of either has never been complete, delinquency studies at the dawn of the 21st century remain heavily focused on measuring delinquency and determining its causes (Gottfredson and Hirschi 1987). In this regard, the positivist ideal of empirical measurement and observation of behavior remains the guidepost of scientific inquiry, but positivistic faith that causes of delinquency beyond the boundaries of the individual can be *changed* has weakened.

Research and policy during the Crime Control Period (1981 to the present) has shown a renewed emphasis on classical principles (e.g., holding juveniles accountable for the choices they make; emphases on deterrence, incapacitation). According to classical views, it is society's responsibility to make sure that perceived costs of crime (as embodied in criminal laws, processing, and punishment) outweigh the benefits, so that a "rational" person will conform because it is in his or her own best interests to do so. Examination of the effects of laws and justice system responses on human behavior is nothing new; it is only the emphasis that changes over time. Classical ideals of rationality and individual accountability have increasingly regained a hold on juvenile justice policy and delinquency research.[3]

At the same time, this particular period witnessed some of the most important developments in delinquency measurement and theory since 1900. Next, we outline several of the major developments during this period.

Improvements in measurement

Multiple measures of delinquency, subjected to higher degrees of scrutiny for reliability and validity, continue to be emphasized. Continued improvements in information systems and collection over time have made it increasingly possible to employ new measures of delinquency and its correlates, to examine linkages between different influences of delinquency, and to monitor intervention process and outcome over time (see Welsh and Harris 1999, ch. 7).

Standardized definitions and measures of youth violence obtained through self-reports are greatly enhancing our ability to make regional comparisons of delinquency and test theories across different sites. In OJJDP's multisite, longitudinal causes and correlates of delinquency study, researchers employ the same core measures across three sites (Denver, Rochester, and Pittsburgh). For each site, researchers collect data on delinquent behavior, drug use, juvenile justice system involvement, community characteristics, family experiences, peer relationships, educational experiences, attitudes and values, and demographic characteristics. Self-report data collected in 1987 and 1988 produced higher estimates of juvenile involvement in violent crime than estimates based on official statistics: 12 to 20 percent of males ages 13 to 16 reported committing acts of serious violence (including aggravated assault, robbery, rape, or gang fights) in the previous year (Kelley et al. 1997).

The National Youth Survey (NYS) has become one of the best known and widely used sources of self-reported delinquency data (Elliott, Huizinga, and Ageton 1985; Elliott, Huizinga, and Menard 1989). NYS is a 5-year panel study of a national probability sample of 1,726 persons ages 11 to 17 in 1976. These adolescents were interviewed in 5 successive years (1977–81), and later at 3-year intervals. Nine waves of data are now available on this panel, whose subjects were ages 27 to 33 when last interviewed in 1993 (Elliott 1994). Both self-report and official record data are available for respondents, and official record data are available for parents or primary caretakers (Elliott 1994). Data are available on a wide variety of variables, including the demographic and socioeconomic status of respondents, parents and friends, neighborhood problems, education, employment, skills, aspirations, encouragement, normlessness, attitudes toward deviance, exposure to delinquent peers, self-reported depression, delinquency, drug and alcohol use, victimization, pregnancy, abortion, use of mental health and outpatient services, violence by respondent and acquaintances, use of controlled drugs, and sexual activity. Important findings regarding delinquency patterns deserve brief attention (see Elliott 1994). For example, females were found to be involved in a much higher proportion of crime than previously estimated by the Uniform Crime Reports (UCR). Although UCR reported eight males to every one female arrested for serious violent crime, NYS found a much smaller gender differential that increased gradually over time: only 2 to 1 at age 12, 3 to 1 by age 18, and 4 to 1 by age 21. Race differentials were also smaller using NYS data. While UCR reported 4 African-American males for every white male arrested for a serious violent crime, NYS reported an offending ratio of only 3:2. NYS also found a much earlier age of onset for violent offending (14–17) than previous estimates provided by official statistics (18–24). NYS has found a consistent progression to more serious acts of delinquency over time. For example, aggravated assault preceded robbery in 85 percent of cases and rape in 92 percent of cases (Elliott 1994).

Developmental and life-course perspectives

Criminologists have often preferred to study differences among groups of offenders, rather than changes in individual offending over time (LeBlanc and Loeber 1998). As a consequence, we know little about changes in individual rates of offending, both increases and decreases, over the life cycle. Similarly, we do not know whether causes are invariant through the life cycle, or whether different sets of causes operate for offenders at different ages, developmental stages, and life transitions. Greater focus on longitudinal measurement of delinquency and its causes fueled greater interest in developmental and life-course theoretical perspectives in the 1990s. Longitudinal research has a rich tradition in criminology (Farrington 1998), and more recent research has focused more on elaborating, integrating, and testing different aspects of the developmental process.

The life course can be defined as pathways through the age-differentiated life span. Researchers are interested in the prevalence, frequency, and onset of offending, as well as different developmental pathways to delinquency. Age differentiation carries different implications for expectations and options, decisional processes, and the course of events that shape critical life stages, transitions, and turning points (Elder 1985). Researchers ask questions such as: How do early childhood characteristics (e.g., antisocial behavior) lead to adult behavioral processes and outcomes? How do life transitions (e.g., shifts in relationships from parents to peers, transitions from same-sex peers to opposite-sex peers, transitions from attending school to beginning work, marriage, divorce, etc.) influence behavior and behavioral choices? How do offending and victimization interact over the life cycle?

Three sets of dynamic concepts are important to this perspective: (1) activation, (2) aggravation, and (3) desistance (LeBlanc and Loeber 1998). Activation refers to the ways that delinquent behaviors, once initiated, are stimulated, and the processes by which the continuity, frequency, and diversity of delinquency are shaped. Three types of activation are possible: (1) acceleration (increased frequency of offending over time), (2) stabilization (increased continuity over time), and (3) diversification (propensity of individuals to become involved in more diverse delinquent activities). Aggravation, the second dynamic process, refers to the existence of a developmental sequence of activities that escalate or increase in seriousness over time. Desistance, the third process, describes a slowing down in the frequency of offending (deceleration), a reduction in its variety (specialization), or a reduction in its seriousness (de-escalation).

This perspective has two distinct foci (LeBlanc and Loeber 1998): (1) a descriptive analysis of the development and dynamics of offending with age, and (2) identification of causal factors that precede or co-occur with behavioral development and influence its course. Researchers thus seek not only to describe the three types of behavioral change listed above, but to identify causal influences of each of the three types of behavior at different ages.

Illustrative of the contributions of this perspective to understanding delinquency is the Pittsburgh Youth Study (Browning and Loeber 1999). The study has followed 1,517 inner-city boys since 1986. Researchers found significant racial differences in serious delinquency, with prevalence at age 16 reaching 27 percent for African-Americans and 19 percent for whites. As prevalence increased, so did the average frequency of serious offending. Onset was also earlier for African-Americans, with 51 percent compared with 28 percent of whites committing serious delinquent acts by age 15. Generally, less serious problem behaviors preceded more serious problem behaviors, although the sequence of life events leading to serious delinquency was not always identical. Researchers identified three major pathways that represented conceptually similar groupings of offenses. The *authority conflict* pathway describes youths who exhibit stubbornness prior to age 12, then move on to defiance and avoidance of authority. The *covert* (or concealing) pathway includes minor covert acts initially, such as lying, followed by property damage and moderate delinquency, then serious delinquency. The *overt* (or confrontive) pathway includes minor aggression followed by fighting and increasing acts of violence. Researchers also examine how different risk factors at the individual, family, and macro levels interact to influence developmental pathways. Although these interactions are complex (e.g., different risk factors become more or less prominent at different ages, and interact with one another in different ways), several patterns can be summarized. Both impulsive judgment and impulsive behavior were significantly, positively related to delinquency, even controlling for differences in IQ and socioeconomic status. However, impulsivity interacted with poverty to increase serious delinquency. In addition, low IQ exerted significant, independent effects on delinquency. Of the family risk factors examined, poor supervision was the strongest predictor of delinquency, followed by poor parent-son communication and physical punishment. The strongest macrolevel predictors were receipt of public assistance (welfare), followed by low socioeconomic status.

As LeBlanc and Loeber (1998) note, the developmental or life-course perspective is building momentum in criminology (see also Thornberry 1997). This approach, they argue, allows for the testing of specific questions critical not only to crime theory but to crime prevention policy. Needless to say, this perspective offers a rich but complex research agenda that is itself in an early but vigorous stage of development.

Risk and protective factors

Other important trends include increased interests in *risk* and *protective* factors and community involvement in delinquency prevention strategies (e.g., Communities that Care, SafeFutures). The risk approach gained momentum during the past 10 to 15 years. Growing out of the public health perspective, risk factors can be defined as statistical or conditional probabilities that are associated with victimization or offending. "Risk" is indicated when certain factors, such as gender (being male), elevate the likelihood of delinquent behavior. "Protection" is indicated when certain factors, such as being raised in a two-parent rather than single-parent family, lower the likelihood of delinquent behavior.

Research has consistently documented certain risk factors for violent juvenile offending (Greenwood 1992; Hawkins and Catalano 1995; Howell 1995; Reiss and Roth 1993; Roth 1994). At the individual level, risk factors include pregnancy and delivery complications, hyperactivity, concentration problems, restlessness, risk-taking behavior, early aggressiveness, early involvement in other forms of antisocial behavior, and beliefs and attitudes favorable to deviant or antisocial behavior. Family factors that increase risk include delinquent siblings, criminal behavior of parents, harsh discipline, physical abuse or neglect, poor family management practices, low levels of parent-child involvement, high levels of family conflict, parental attitudes favorable to violence, and separation of the child from family. School factors associated with higher risk include academic failure, low commitment to education, truancy, early dropout, frequent changes of schools, association with delinquent peers, and gang membership. Community or neighborhood risk factors include high population density, high residential mobility, high poverty rate, availability of weapons and drugs, and high rate of adult involvement in crime.

The prototypical risk-based approach, the Social Development Strategy (Catalano and Hawkins 1996; Hawkins and Catalano 1992; Howell 1995), has been widely applied and adapted to juvenile justice and human services settings. In fact, OJJDP adopted this approach as the foundation for its *Comprehensive Strategy for Serious, Violent, and Chronic Juvenile Offenders* (Wilson and Howell 1993). According to this approach, delinquency and substance abuse can be reduced by enhancing known protective factors. Healthy beliefs and clear standards for behavior in the family, school, and community (i.e., "protective" factors) directly promote healthy behavior in children. By encouraging bonding with people and institutions (families, peer groups, schools, and communities) that promote healthy beliefs and clear standards, the model suggests, youths will be encouraged to adopt similar beliefs and standards. Individual characteristics (e.g., prosocial orientation, intelligence, resilient temperament) affect a child's ability to perceive opportunities, learn skills, and obtain recognition. The Social Development Strategy is directly derived from control theory and social learning theory (Catalano and Hawkins 1996; Hawkins and Catalano 1992).

Many delinquency prevention programs have been based on this approach (Howell 1995). For example, community-based delinquency prevention programs promote bonding to prosocial individuals and institutions by providing opportunities, skills, and recognition (Welsh, Jenkins, and Harris 1999). Programs:

- Stress the value of supervised activities to keep youths out of trouble.

- Provide some form of life skills training (e.g., problem-solving skills, conflict resolution, and cultural diversity and awareness training).

- Provide homework or tutoring assistance.

- Offer structured recreation and/or field trips.

- Provide career development or vocational training.

- Often include a community service component.

Despite abundant evidence that crime is related to time, place, culture, and social structure, delinquency research over the past century has heavily emphasized individual offenders' motivations.

Some risk factors can be modified to reduce the odds of specific acts or events occurring. There is always a chance, however, that delinquency will still occur in a low-risk setting or fail to occur in a very high-risk setting. Risk factors are statistical probabilities, not predetermined certainties, when applied to any individual case. The risk approach, like its public health ancestor, focuses mainly on prevention. Explanation is not its primary purpose, however, and many have criticized the risk approach as atheoretical (Moore 1995).

Those who advocate a risk-focused approach are informed by etiological research, although they are more directly concerned with identifying risk factors that are malleable through ethical and humane methods (see Hawkins and Catalano 1992). If one were dedicated to reducing the spread of a contagious disease such as smallpox, for example, one would certainly be interested in the etiology of that disease. That knowledge would prove extremely useful in lowering risk, perhaps by developing a vaccine to attack the specific viral agent involved. Indeed, part of the logic for a *useful* theory or a *useful* risk factor is whether interventions based on its logic will work (Moore 1995).

Risk factors, therefore, offer clues for explanation; they are empirical patterns to be explained. Any useful theory must be capable of *explaining* the statistical or conditional probabilities identified by research (see Braithwaite 1989). Both types of research are useful: Theory focuses more on etiology; risk approach focuses more on prevention.

Multilevel and interactional approaches to delinquency

Greater sophistication of information and computing systems has also begun to spur interest in testing *multilevel* (contextual) theories of delinquency (i.e., examining the relative explanatory power of individual, institutional, social structural, and cultural factors associated with delinquency). Despite abundant evidence that crime is related to time, place, culture, and social structure, delinquency research over the past century has heavily emphasized individual offenders' motivations. Calls for multilevel approaches and "integrated" theories have become more frequent in recent years.

The National Academy of Sciences panel on the Understanding and Causes of Violent Behavior, composed of an international panel of experts from a variety of disciplines, was established in 1989 to review existing knowledge and make recommendations to control violence (Reiss and Roth 1993). One of its main conclusions was that we have many promising directions for intervention and prevention to pursue from research findings, but better measures and more controlled research, especially evaluations of promising efforts, are needed to identify causes and opportunities for prevention. Using the risk approach to classify different predictors, panel members proposed a matrix consisting of two main dimensions: *temporal proximity* (closeness in time) of a predictor to the violent event, and the *level of analysis* at which that predictor is observed.

Levels of analysis refer to different units of observation and analysis, including macrosocial, microsocial, psychosocial, and biological (neurobehavioral). Macrosocial factors are characteristics (e.g., poverty, unemployment) of large social units such as communities, cities, States, and countries. Macrosocial predictors include both social structural and cultural variables. Microsocial factors are characteristics of encounters among people (e.g., family and group dynamics, situational factors such as availability of weapons, organizational and institutional processes). Psychosocial factors include individual characteristics (e.g., personality, learned rewards) or temporary states (e.g., influence of alcohol, stress) that influence interactions with others. Biological or neurobehavioral factors, primarily in the brain, include chemical, electrical, and hormonal influences on behavior. Consistent with the risk approach, panel members suggested that prevention and intervention depend on breaking some link in the chain of events preceding the violent act. There are multiple options for intervening, and greater need for interagency collaboration: "[V]iolence problem-solving will require long-term collaboration and new organizational arrangements among local law enforcement, criminal justice, schools, and public health, emergency medicine, and social service agencies, all working with program evaluators and other researchers" (Reiss and Roth 1993, 10).

The multilevel approach carries important implications for the study of delinquency and youth gangs (Short 1998). First, juvenile delinquency is largely a group phenomenon, and the influence of gangs on individual members requires more detailed study of group processes and dynamics—not just individuals in groups—than has been the case. Second, there is a need for more precise definitions and classifications of "gangs" that separate gang membership from gang behavior. Such research would elaborate the processes and conditions under which groups form, become delinquent, and develop different norms of behavior, some delinquent and some nondelinquent. Third, the study of delinquency and youth gangs would benefit greatly from development of a viable typology that situates gangs or "youth networks" in a larger set of youth collectivities.

Such discussion inevitably leads to talk about theoretical integration. Some argue that efforts to support or falsify distinct theories should continue; others argue that different theories are not mutually exclusive at all and can be profitably integrated in some cases (e.g., Bernard and Snipes 1996). Theory, according to this latter view, should direct research and accumulate its product into a coherent, understandable product. Such is the aim of scientific progress. However, the failure to do so is witnessed by a million modest studies that produce a million conflicting results.

Although Bernard and Snipes give only passing attention to emerging statistical models such as hierarchical linear modeling, where independent variables can easily cross at least three levels of explanation (e.g., individual, institutional, and community),[4] they agree in their conclusion that "multilevel explanations of individual criminal behavior, using a contextual approach, seem both desirable and feasible" (1996, 343). They conclude that more integrated theories are possible, and more complicated contextual theories that locate individual behavior within various groups, settings, social structures, and cultures are badly needed. The near future will likely witness an explosion of interest and growth in multilevel, contextual theories.

Juvenile Crime: Patterns and Changes Over Time

Based on measures of delinquency over time, we explore in this section major changes, or continuities, in delinquency seriousness (e.g., violent versus property crime), types (e.g., gang, drug, school, and firearm-related violence), and frequency (e.g., ratios of juvenile to adult offenders for different crimes, juvenile arrest and victimization rates for different crimes). Shifts in juvenile crime involvement will be explored, with an emphasis on the past 30 years.

According to the FBI, law enforcement agencies in the United States arrested 2.8 million juveniles in 1997. Of all juvenile arrests, only 123,000, 4.4 percent, were for Index violent crime offenses (murder, forcible rape, robbery, or aggravated assault).

Widely used official measures of delinquency include UCR collected by the Federal Bureau of Investigation (FBI) since 1930. Submission of data by police departments was initially voluntary, but 44 States enacted mandatory reporting legislation by 1997. Part I offenses, or "Index" offenses, include murder and nonnegligent homicide, forcible rape, aggravated assault, and robbery. Part II offenses include drug abuse violations, simple assaults, drunkenness, and disorderly conduct. UCR limitations have been reviewed extensively elsewhere (e.g., Biderman and Lynch 1991; Gove, Hughes, and Geerken 1985; Reiss and Roth 1993, appendix B).

Changes in delinquency types and seriousness

We begin by emphasizing two critical but often overlooked facts: (1) property crimes such as burglary or theft outnumber violent crimes by a ratio of at least 3 to 1, and (2) adult offenders outnumber juvenile offenders by a ratio of nearly 5 to 1 for Index violent crimes and nearly 2 to 1 for Index property crimes (Maguire and Pastore 1999). The percentage of crimes committed by juveniles relative to adults decreased between 1971 and 1997 for both property crimes (51 percent in 1971 versus 35 percent in 1997) and violent crimes (23 percent in 1971 versus 19 percent in 1997). We further examine delinquency shifts and evidence below.

According to the FBI, law enforcement agencies in the United States arrested 2.8 million juveniles in 1997 (Snyder 1998). Of all juvenile arrests, only 123,000, 4.4 percent, were for Index violent crime offenses (murder, forcible rape, robbery, or aggravated assault).

The vast majority of juvenile arrests are for property offenses, and for all offenses except arson, juveniles commit a much smaller proportion of offenses than adults (see exhibit 1). This is not to argue that juveniles never commit serious acts of violence, only that violent crimes committed by juveniles should be placed in a broader context. In 1997, juveniles accounted for 30 percent of robbery arrests, 17 percent of forcible rape arrests, 14 percent of aggravated assault arrests, and 14 percent of all murder arrests (Snyder 1998).

Exhibit 1. Juvenile proportion of arrests by offense, 1997

Offense	Percent juvenile*
All arrests	19
Index violent	17
Index property	35
Arson	50
Vandalism	43
Motor vehicle theft	40
Burglary	37
Larceny-theft	34
Robbery	30
Disorderly conduct	27
Stolen property	25
Liquor laws	25
Weapon	24
Sex offense	18
Other assault	17
Forcible rape	17
Murder	14
Aggravated assault	14
Drug abuse	14
Vagrancy	11
Fraud	3
Drunkenness	3
Prostitution	1
DUI	1

* Juveniles are defined as all persons under age 18.

Note: The Violent Crime Index includes the offenses of murder and nonnegligent manslaughter, forcible rape, robbery, and aggravated assault. The Property Crime Index includes the offenses of burglary, larceny-theft, motor vehicle theft, and arson. Running away from home and curfew violations are not presented in this figure because, by definition, only juveniles can be arrested for these offenses.

Source: Snyder, Howard. *Juvenile proportion of arrests by offense, 1997.* Adapted from Snyder 1998. Retrieved 3 January 2000 from the World Wide Web: http://ojjdp.ncjrs.org/ojstatbb/qa003.html.

Data Source: U.S. Department of Justice, Federal Bureau of Investigation. 1998. *Crime in the United States 1997.* Uniform Crime Reports. Washington, D.C. Table 38.

In exhibit 2, we see changes in arrest rates for violent crime since 1970. Exhibit 2 shows sharp increases in violent offending rates for ages 15 to 24 between 1986 and 1994, with declines beginning in 1995. Using UCR arrest figures as a reference point, adults ages 18 to 20 have had the highest rates of involvement in violent crime over time, closely followed by juveniles in the 15 to 17 age group and adults in the 21 to 24 age group. These trends are based on arrest *rates*, however, which are calculated by dividing the number of offenses

Exhibit 2. Arrest rates for violent Index offenses per 100,000 population, by age group, 1970–97

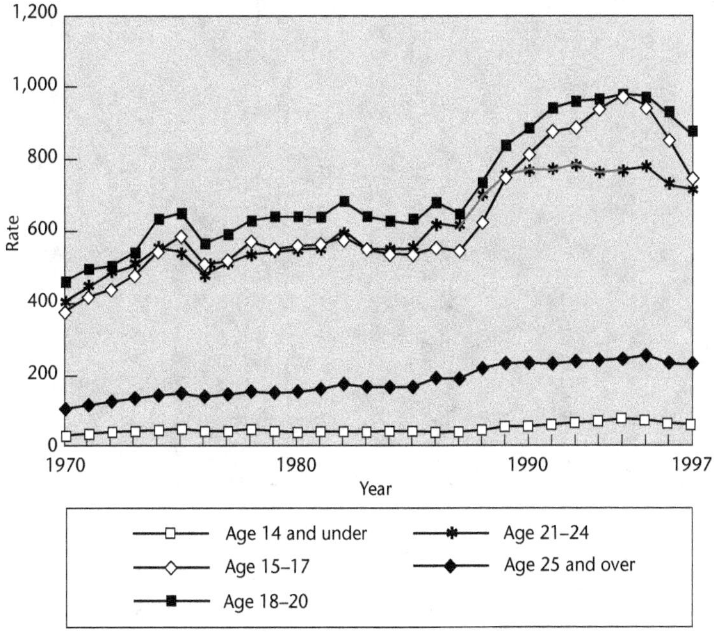

Note: The Violent Crime Index includes the offenses of murder and nonnegligent manslaughter, forcible rape, robbery, and aggravated assault.

Source: U.S. Department of Justice, Bureau of Justice Statistics. 1999. Arrests by age group, number, and rates for total offenses, Index offenses, violent offenses, and property offenses, 1970–97. Spreadsheet. *Crime and justice electronic data abstracts*. Retrieved 3 January 2000 from the World Wide Web: http://www.ojp.usdoj.gov/bjs/dtdata.htm.

committed by people in each age group by the total population in each age group. These rates give a good idea of how common violent offending is within each age group, but they do not necessarily indicate the total volume of offenders being processed by justice agencies. Both types of measures are important.

The total volume of violent crime committed by juveniles is relatively small. In exhibit 3, we see that arrests of violent offenders ages 25 and over far outnumber arrests for any other age group. The same age group displays the sharpest

Exhibit 3. Number of arrests for violent Index offenses, by age group, 1970–97

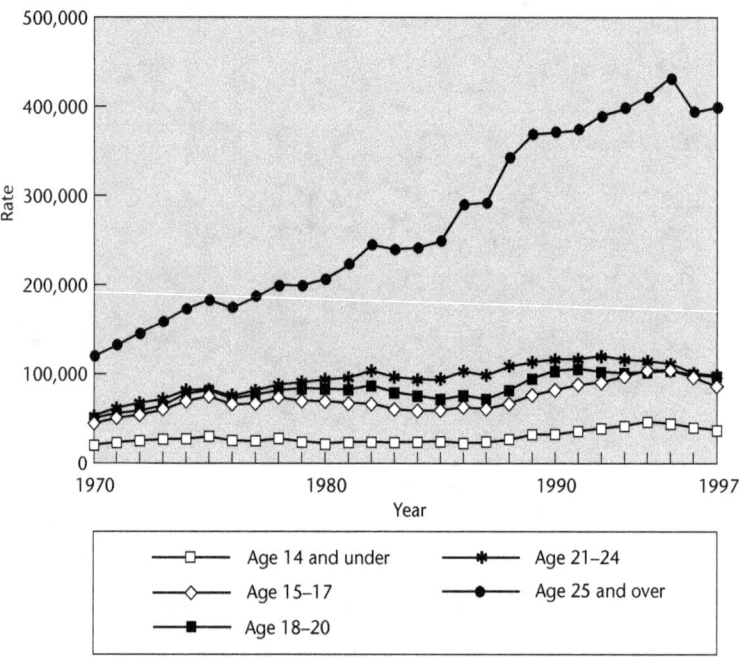

Note: The Violent Crime Index includes the offenses of murder and nonnegligent manslaughter, forcible rape, robbery, and aggravated assault.

Source: U.S. Department of Justice, Bureau of Justice Statistics. 1999. Arrests by age group, number, and rates for total offenses, Index offenses, violent offenses, and property offenses, 1970–97. Spreadsheet. *Crime and justice electronic data abstracts.* Retrieved 3 January 2000 from the World Wide Web: http://www.ojp.usdoj.gov/bjs/dtdata.htm.

increase in arrests for violent offending over time, although other age groups show much smaller increases between 1986 and 1994 before declining in 1995. Juveniles are arrested for violent offenses in much lower numbers than adults, with those ages 15 to 17 arrested in numbers comparable to, but still slightly lower than, those in the 18 to 20 and 21 to 24 age groups.

We find similar patterns for property crimes. Exhibit 4 shows arrest rates for Index property crimes. According to exhibit 4, juvenile offenders in the age group 15 to 17 commit property offenses at the highest rate of the five age groups examined. Again, however, we emphasize that such statistics are meaningful only

Exhibit 4. Arrest rates for property Index offenses, per 100,000 population, by age group, 1970–97

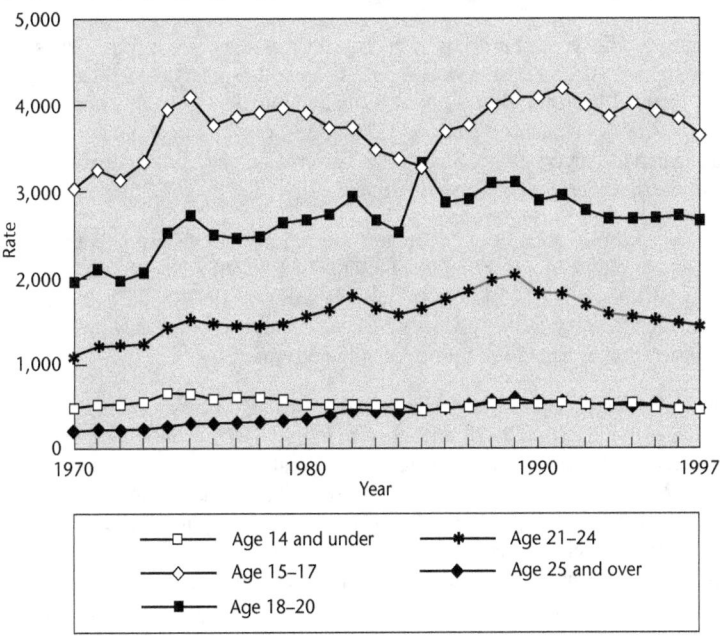

Note: The Property Crime Index includes the offenses of burglary, larceny-theft, motor vehicle theft, and arson.

Source: U.S. Department of Justice, Bureau of Justice Statistics. 1999. Arrests by age group, number, and rates for total offenses, index offenses, violent offenses, and property offenses, 1970–97. Spreadsheet. *Crime and justice electronic data abstracts.* Retrieved 3 January 2000 from the World Wide Web: http://www.ojp.usdoj.gov/bjs/dtdata.htm.

to the degree that they reveal which age group contains the highest proportion of property offenders. We need to probe further to see who commits the greatest numbers of property crimes.

As we see in exhibit 5, serious property crimes are committed disproportionately by those in the 25 and over age group. This particular age group shows the greatest increases over time, although Index property crimes overall are down since 1994. Those ages 15 to 17 commit a higher number of property crimes than those ages 18 to 20 and 21 to 24, however, and even juveniles ages 14 and under commit a slightly higher number of property crimes than those ages 21 to 24. Although juveniles are involved in much less crime overall than adults, property crimes are where they show up in the highest numbers. Overall, though, property crimes committed by juveniles changed little between 1970 and 1994, and have decreased since then.

Some specific types of property crime have increased, however, while others have decreased. The total number of arrests for both burglary (–15 percent) and car theft (–17 percent) decreased substantially from 1988 to 1997, while arrests for larceny (+9 percent) and arson (+22 percent) were up somewhat for the same period (Snyder 1999). Since 1980, however, burglary is the only one of the four Index property offenses to decrease.

Other non-Index offenses (e.g., simple assaults, forgery, vandalism, drug abuse violations, liquor law violations, and disorderly conduct) accounted for a whopping 54.4 percent (1,545,400) of all juvenile arrests in 1997 (Snyder 1999). Juvenile offenders, as they always have been, are disproportionately involved in property crimes and in less serious (non-Index) crimes.

If we focus for a moment only on non-Index offenses where the number of offenses has increased by 20 percent or more from 1988 to 1997, we find large increases in arrests for simple assaults (84 percent), fraud (58 percent), vandalism (20 percent), weapons carrying or possession (44 percent), drug abuse violations (125 percent), gambling (166 percent), offenses against the family and children (150 percent), and disorderly conduct (86 percent). The only non-Index offenses that have decreased by 20 percent or more are prostitution and commercialized vice (–28 percent) and driving under the influence (–21 percent) (Snyder 1999).

So-called "status" offenses (suspicion, curfew and loitering, and runaways) made up the remaining 468,000 (16.5 percent) of the total number of juvenile arrests in 1997 (Snyder 1998), and curfew violations and runaways made up the majority (99.7 percent) of arrests in this category.

Exhibit 5. Number of arrests for property Index offenses, by age group, 1970–97

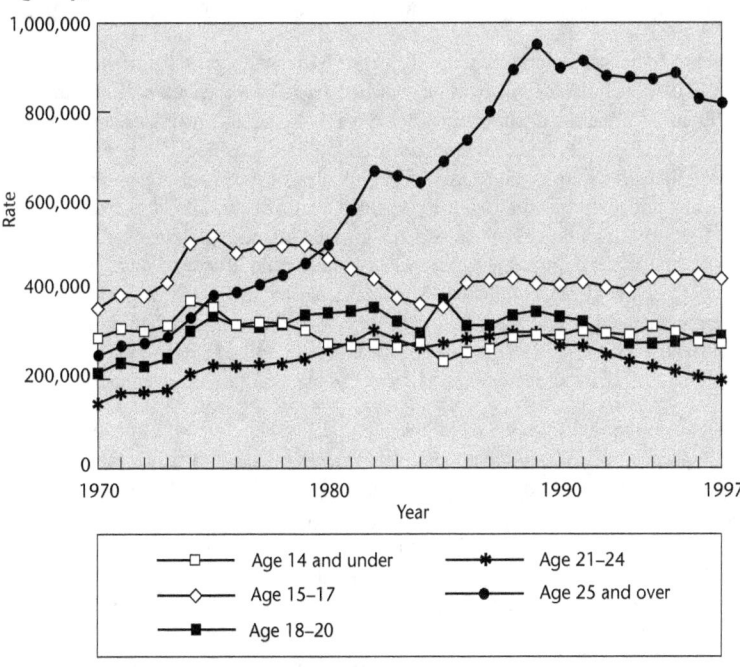

Note: The Property Crime Index includes the offenses of burglary, larceny-theft, motor vehicle theft, and arson.

Source: U.S. Department of Justice, Bureau of Justice Statistics. 1999. Arrests by age group, number, and rates for total offenses, Index offenses, violent offenses, and property offenses, 1970–97. Spreadsheet. *Crime and justice electronic data abstracts.* Retrieved 3 January 2000 from the World Wide Web: http://www.ojp.usdoj.gov/bjs/dtdata.htm.

Given the relatively low involvement of juveniles in both property and violent crime relative to their adult counterparts, how then do we explain the toughened policy response to juvenile offenders in the last two decades of the 20th century? We believe that very short-term shifts in violent crime, especially homicide, largely drove the get-tough policy on juvenile offenders since the 1980s.

After more than a decade of relative stability, juvenile violent crime arrests began to increase in the 1980s, peaking in 1994. In fact, in 1994, teens ages 15 to 17 exceeded the *arrest rate* for Index violent crime offenses of adults ages 18 to 20. But things began to change in 1995 when juvenile arrests for Index violent crime offenses continued to decline for 3 years in a row (exhibits 2 and 3).

Exhibit 6 shows the number of murders known to involve juvenile offenders since 1980. Homicides involving juvenile offenders increased dramatically from 1988 to 1994, before declining in 1995. Note, however, that juveniles committed only a small proportion of all homicides, and this remains true over time. In 1980, juveniles were involved in 1,283 homicides, or 8 percent of the total. These numbers declined through 1984, when there were about 800 homicides, or 5 percent of all homicides, in which a juvenile offender was involved. After 1984, homicides by juveniles grew both in number and in proportion to the whole (Snyder 1998). Homicides by juveniles peaked in 1994 when juveniles were implicated in 2,317 homicides, 16 percent of the total, and then dropped substantially between 1994 and 1995. Juveniles committed only 1,545 (13.5 percent) of 11,475 known homicides in 1997, the most recent year available.

We do not argue that increases in juvenile violence between 1988 and 1994 are unimportant, only that some broader perspective is needed. In 1997, the juvenile arrest rate for murder was 20 percent above the 1988 rate, but 40 percent lower than in 1993. The juvenile arrest rate for forcible rape changed little from 1983 through 1997, while the 1997 rate was 23 percent below the peak year of 1991 (Snyder 1998). Juvenile robbery arrests declined 30 percent from 1980 through 1988, then increased 70 percent between 1988 and 1994. The juvenile robbery rate declined substantially for the next 3 years, nearly reaching its lowest level in 20 years (Snyder 1998). Juvenile arrests for aggravated assault showed huge increases from 1983 to 1994 (120 percent). Similar increases (+135 percent) were observed for simple assaults. However, the rate of juvenile arrests for aggravated assault fell 16 percent between 1994 and 1997, while the juvenile arrest rate for simple assault continued to increase (+9 percent). Needless to say, current levels of juvenile violence are still above 1970 or 1980 rates (see exhibits 2 and 3), and recent decreases leave little cause for celebration or complacency (Snyder 1998). However, what seems clear is that responses to juvenile crime have toughened much more than can be explained by increased juvenile involvement in crime. This is true even if we focus on an extremely small proportion of offenses (e.g., homicide or robbery), for offenders (e.g., ages 15 to 17), for a limited time period (1988–94).

If attention is drawn to serious, violent delinquency, rather than the more frequent property crimes and adult offenders, policymakers and the public are inevitably drawn to a juvenile underworld of guns, gangs, drugs, and violence. Although important, such phenomena are still relatively uncommon. To the

Exhibit 6. Number of murders known to involve juvenile offenders, 1980–95

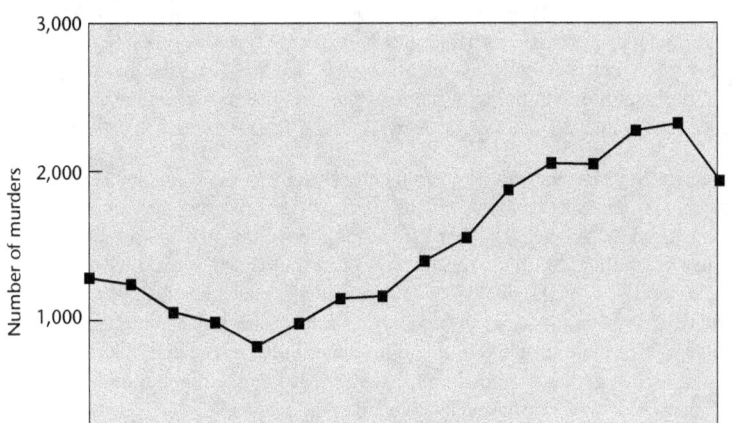

Source: Snyder, Howard. Murders known to involve juvenile offenders, 1980–1995. *OJJDP Statistical Briefing Book*. Retrieved 3 January 2000 from the World Wide Web: http://ojjdp.ncjrs. org/ojstatbb/qa051.html

Data Source: Author's analysis of the Federal Bureau of Investigation's Supplementary Homicide Reports 1980–1995 [machine-readable data files], 1997.

degree that Federal funding agencies adopt these foci as priorities for legislation and funding, a potentially misleading research agenda is created. Social scientists aspire to influence policy, but policymakers also shape the types of research studies that get funded and completed (Hagan 1989). If we keep in mind that property crimes occur much more frequently than violent crimes, and that juveniles commit only a small proportion of all crimes, we will keep delinquency in a more accurate perspective.

Juvenile gangs and drug-related crime

Juvenile gangs have existed throughout the 20th century, with excellent accounts provided by Chicago School sociologists such as Thrasher (1927) and Whyte (1943). However, increases in gang membership, gang activity, and gang-related violence since the 1980s have caused renewed concern. In particular, gangs have become more involved in drug activity (but by no means drug activity exclusively) and are more likely to possess, carry, or use firearms than in the past. Recent research studies consistently indicate that gang activity has extended beyond large urban areas into suburban and rural areas, and that gangs are increasingly diverse in terms of ethnic composition, organization, and involvement in delinquent or criminal activities (e.g., Curry, Ball, and Decker 1996; Klein 1995).

Changes in gangs have occurred with rapid changes in the social and economic structure of cities and suburbs (Fagan 1996). In particular, two factors have fundamentally changed the labor market for poor young men and women in urban areas since 1970: (1) replacement of unskilled and semiskilled blue-collar jobs with "pink-collar" jobs requiring higher educational and skill levels, and (2) growth of the informal economy, especially illegitimate drug markets. Changes in legitimate markets, therefore, shaped illegitimate opportunities, and social control in neighborhoods, already weakened by the flight of middle-class residents, was further weakened by volatile drug markets.

Deindustrialization has altered the nature of gangs, creating new relationships among gangs, illegal drug distribution, and the survival of young adult gang members in a postindustrial, segmented economy (Hagedorn 1991). Hagedorn described deteriorating neighborhoods with declining resources and fractured internal cohesion. Neighborhoods were characterized not by the absence of working people, but rather by the absence of effective social institutions.

Based on fieldwork in New York City's Spanish Harlem district, Bourgois (1997) argued that a culture of resistance and an underground economy emerged in opposition to demeaning, underpaid employment. Regular displays of violence became necessary for success in the underground economy. Employers looked for individuals who could demonstrate a capacity for effective violence and terror. Violence became a tool not just for drug dealers, but for others who wanted to maintain a sense of autonomy and dignity. Interacting cultural and structural influences, according to this perspective, are an ideological dynamic of ethnic discrimination that interacts explosively with an economic dynamic of class exploitation, a concept Bourgois terms "conjugated oppression."

However, many unanswered questions remain about these new types of gangs (Short 1998). For example, what criteria should be used to classify gangs into types? How do gangs relate to drug crews, milling crowds, delinquent networks, skinheads, bikers, and many other groups in which youths participate? How do gangs relate to friendship groups and processes that begin long before adolescence? A renewed and vigorous research agenda focused on juvenile gangs is needed in the 21st century.

School disorder and violence

Schools are primary settings for juvenile violence. Thirty-seven percent of all violent crimes experienced by youths ages 12 to 15 occurred on school grounds (Whitaker and Bastian 1991), while 56 percent of all juvenile victimizations (property and violent crimes) in 1991 occurred in school or on school property. Snyder and Sickmund (1995, 16) explain that "There is no comparable place where crimes against adults were so concentrated."

Increased research and policy attention will continue for some time to be devoted to measuring, explaining, and preventing school violence, largely in response to a few dramatic, bloody incidents such as the Littleton, Colorado, high school massacre on April 20, 1999, and the Jonesboro, Arkansas, schoolyard shootings on March 24, 1998. While public perceptions of any social problem are frequently driven by such rare incidents (Welsh and Harris 1999), there is still cause for concern.

A National School Board Association survey of 720 school districts throughout the United States found that 39 percent of urban school districts use metal detectors, 64 percent use locker searches, and 65 percent use security personnel in their schools (National School Board Association 1993). In the same survey, 82 percent of school districts reported that the problem of school violence is worse now than it was 5 years ago. Overall, 35 percent believed that school violence had increased significantly and that the incidents were more serious.

Results from the 1995 National Crime Victimization Survey, based on interviews conducted with a nationally representative sample of more than 10,000 youths, showed that 14.5 percent of students ages 12 to 19 experienced one or more violent or property crimes at school over a 6-month period (Chandler et al. 1998), with the percentage of youths reporting violent victimizations increasing from 3.4 percent in 1989 to 4.2 percent in 1995. The percentage of students reporting a street gang presence at their school nearly doubled to 28.4 percent between 1989 and 1995 (Chandler et al. 1998), and those who reported the presence of gangs at their school were twice as likely to fear attack (Bastian and Taylor 1991). Unfortunately, the risk of being either a victim or perpetrator of violent crime is much greater for children attending school in poor, urban, minority communities (Sheley, McGee, and Wright 1995).

Misbehavior of low-income, African-American children may partially represent reactions to oppressive life experiences and standards perceived as unfair and unobtainable (Cohen 1955), resulting in attempts to recapture feelings of self-worth, identity, and respect by adopting norms of social distancing and physical toughness (Anderson 1998; Hanna 1988). School and community factors play a role in school violence, however. Welsh, Stokes, and Greene (in press) found that school climate (measured by student attendance and turnover) strongly mediated the effects of community variables (poverty, residential stability, and community crime rate) on school disorder (as measured by school incident and dismissal rates). Poverty retained a significant, indirect effect through its influence on school climate (see also Welsh, Greene, and Jenkins 1999; and Welsh [in press]). Further research is needed to accurately measure school violence; sort out the interactive influences of individual, school, and community-level variables on behavior; and inform the development of effective strategies for violence prevention.

Several other victimization surveys designed specifically for juveniles have been conducted in schools, although space limitations preclude discussion here (but see Anderson 1998; Gottfredson and Gottfredson 1985; Welsh, Greene, and Jenkins 1998; Welsh, Jenkins, and Greene 1997). Delinquency research and theory could benefit considerably by further examining juvenile behavior more closely in natural settings where children spend the most time (e.g., Bursik 1988; Messner and Rosenfeld 1997; Welsh, Greene, and Jenkins 1999).

Firearm-related crime

We cannot examine juvenile violence in the United States without examining the availability and use of guns. Reliable long-term statistics on juvenile gun use are scarce, but official statistics since 1980 provide a chilling picture (Snyder 1998). Juvenile arrests for weapon law violations doubled between 1987 and 1993. Gun homicides by juveniles in the United States tripled between 1983 and 1997, while homicides involving other weapons declined. From 1983 through 1995, the proportion of homicides in which a juvenile used a gun increased from 55 percent to 80 percent (Greenbaum 1997). In fact, the overall increase in juvenile homicide witnessed in the mid-1980s *was* entirely firearm related (Snyder, Sickmund, and Poe-Yamagata 1996). Correspondingly, recent decreases in juvenile homicides are entirely attributable to decreases in murders committed with firearms (Snyder 1998). Perhaps recent law enforcement programs and gun violence prevention programs aimed at juveniles are having some effect (Snyder 1998).

According to the Centers for Disease Control and Prevention (CDC) (U.S. Department of Health and Human Services 1995), 2.5 million teenagers in the United States carry weapons and frequently take them to school. Every day, CDC estimates, 135,000 students bring guns to school. In a 1995 survey of students from 10 inner-city high schools, nearly half of the male students said they could borrow a gun from friends or family if they wanted to, and 40 percent of students said they have a male relative who carries a gun (Sheley and Wright 1993).

In a survey of 758 male students in inner-city high schools and 835 male, serious offenders incarcerated in six detention facilities, Sheley and Wright (1993) found that 83 percent of inmates and 22 percent of students possessed guns. These firearms tended to be high-quality, powerful revolvers. Most detainees and students stated it was easy to acquire a gun; only 35 percent said it would be difficult. Fifty-three percent of students said they would "borrow" a gun from family members or friends if they needed one; 37 percent of students and 54 percent of detainees said they would get one off the street. Though involvement in drug sales was more common among those reporting gun carrying, the main reason given for carrying a gun was self-protection.

Projections of delinquency

Dramatic increases in high-risk juvenile populations and violent juvenile crime have been projected into the 21st century, prompting some to sound an alarm about the coming wave of teenage "superpredators." Prior to recent decreases in 1994, some researchers warned that if trends continued as they had for the past 10 years, juvenile arrests for violent crime would more than double by the year 2010 (Fox 1996; DiIulio 1996).

However, contrary to these predictions, juveniles contributed less than most other age groups to the increase in violent crime arrests between 1980 and 1997. The violent crime arrest rate for juveniles was 22 percent above the rate in 1980, but the rate increases for nearly all other age groups were greater (with the greatest increases, 66 percent and 60 percent, in the 35 to 39 and 30 to 34 age groups, respectively). The increase in juvenile arrests between 1980 and 1997 is not attributable to juvenile involvement in crime in any systematic way (Snyder 1998).

Some have raised concern that juvenile violence will increase in the next 10 to 15 years because the juvenile population is projected to increase at the rate of about 1 percent per year. Fox (1996), for example, noted that the rate of murder committed by adolescents ages 14 to 17 increased 172 percent from 1985 to 1994. The largest increases involved offenders who were friends and acquaintances of their victims. These increases in violent juvenile crime occurred while the population of teenagers was declining. Fox suggested that this demographic trend would soon change, because 39 million children were under age 10 and would soon enter their "high risk" years. Therefore, he concluded, the country would probably experience a future wave of youth violence that would be even worse than the 10 years prior to 1994.

Changes in the size of the juvenile population, however, appear largely unrelated to juvenile violent crime trends in recent years (Snyder 1998; see also

Blumstein et al. 1998). In fact, as we noted above, the rate of juvenile violent crime arrests decreased from 1994 to 1997 at the same time as the juvenile population increased. From 1987 to 1994, the juvenile population increased 7 percent, and juvenile arrests for violent crime increased 79 percent. From 1994 to 1997, juvenile arrests dropped 18 percent, but the juvenile population increased 4 percent. Violent juvenile crime has now declined 3 years in a row (1994–97).

How do we then explain these very recent but compelling decreases in juvenile violence? Blumstein et al. (1998) note that recent (1997) homicide rates remain high, but decreases have been recorded since 1991, when a peak rate of 9.8 per 100,000 was recorded. These authors ask how much this trend is related to age groups, weapons, and city size? Where are the decreases largest, and why? They conclude that changes in the use of weapons are most important in understanding recent peaks and valleys in homicide, particularly juvenile homicide. The growth in homicides by young people from 1985 to 1993 was entirely due to homicides committed with handguns. Recent decreases are similarly due to decreases in handgun-related homicides. These trends are most pronounced for large cities and may be related to the rise and fall of large crack markets and violent drug-related competition in large cities.

It is also possible that recent decreases in violent juvenile crime may be partially due to economic upturn (reduced unemployment rates), police crackdowns on illegal markets, increased incarceration rates (though incapacitation is more of an explanation for decreases in crime committed by older adults), increased youth involvement in legitimate labor markets, and less involvement in illegitimate opportunities. However, it is extremely difficult to parcel out the specific causes of the decrease (e.g., changes in demography, related social behaviors such as drug selling, expansion of police resources). Probably all played some role in interaction with one another. Blumstein et al. (1998) argue that those who would credit police strategies for large declines in crime in New York City have little evidence for their claims. Why was there a steady decline in nongun homicides, they asked, long before Mayor Rudolph Giuliani and former Police Commissioner William Bratton took office and began their multifaceted war on crime?

Curtis (1998) suggests that many people had written off inner cities at the peak of the crack problem in the late 1980s and early 1990s. How do we then explain the sudden decline in violent crime in such places? Curtis refers to ethnographic research in two New York City neighborhoods to look for answers. He suggests that many youths began to withdraw from public life as violence around them increased. He further suggests that two large gangs expanded their control over neighborhoods, but actively campaigned against drug distribution, and instead encouraged youths to build positive lives. Curtis seems to suggest that community activism against violence also played a role, even though economic vitality can hardly be said to have increased markedly. At the same time, long prison sentences and aggressive policing against drug gangs helped reduce the influence of corporate-style drug gangs: many downsized, many disbanded. Remaining distributors became much more discreet and moved indoors, and turf battles were eliminated.

LaFree (1998) notes that violent crime rates increased dramatically from 1963 to 1974. In contrast, recent drops in violent crime are the greatest decreases since World War II. Social institutions provide a promising explanation for recent decreases (e.g., mutually shared and reinforced patterns of norms, rules, and laws). Institutions are capable of changing dramatically over time, and can thus explain huge, rapid decreases in crime. In the peaceful post-World War II years, social institutions (political, economic, and family) were strong. In the 1970s, public trust in political institutions plummeted; economic inequality, inflation, and decline of labor unions all reduced confidence in economic institutions. The traditional family of the 1950s was severely weakened in the 1970s (e.g., both parents working, more single parents, higher divorce rates). American society fought back against institutional decline by investing heavily in other institutions, especially criminal justice, education, and welfare. All three put downward pressure on crime rates, LaFree suggests.

Advocates of the superpredator thesis continue to warn that the country's largest and most violent cohort of young males will soon reach its crime-prone years (DiIulio 1997). In fact, DiIulio argues that the only reason crime has dropped rather than risen since 1994 is because smarter law enforcement (e.g., computer-assisted information systems) and tougher sentencing policies (e.g., policies that keep violent and repeat criminals behind bars) have been successful. Previous research has not confirmed these arguments, but DiIulio argues that there has never been a rigorous, clear-cut test of the association between the visible presence of police and crime rates.

The superpredator thesis so far seems suspect. Projections of crime trends based on straight-line projections of short-term trends (i.e., 1986–94) and single predictors (size of the at-risk youth population) tend not to be very reliable (Moore and Tonry 1998; Zimring and Hawkins 1998). Cook and Laub (1998) demonstrate that little relationship exists between the homicide count for youths ages 13 to 17 and their population count since 1968. They note that our ability to predict youth violence is limited by incomplete understanding of its various determinants, and the recent volatility in youth violence since the mid-1980s demonstrates that "making confident predictions is a fool's game" (Cook and Laub 1998, 58).

The Changing Social, Economic, and Cultural Context

An understanding of the forces shaping juvenile justice policy requires an examination of the larger context in which delinquency, juvenile justice policy, and the evolving juvenile justice system are embedded. The juvenile court was created during a time when several contextual forces were interacting: urban areas had been growing rapidly, numbers of first-generation immigrants were especially great, biologically based theories were shaping the thinking of those in power, and the roles played by women outside of the home were changing. The origins of the juvenile court have been attributed to a desire to save children from undesirable life circumstances (Platt 1977), a desire to exercise greater control over lower class ruffians, and a perceived need on the part of prosecutors and the police to correct a situation in which young offenders were being acquitted by sympathetic juries (Mennel 1973).

Structural shifts in the juvenile justice system that occurred during the Juvenile Rights Period (1961–80) are also best understood if viewed in terms of the social and cultural context of that time. Civil unrest and significant court activity in the area of civil rights lay the groundwork for examining and specifying the rights of juveniles. *In re Gault* and other due process cases of this era gave rise to a more adversarial court that has had both positive benefits and unanticipated negative consequences for juvenile justice.

At the beginning of the 21st century, the juvenile justice system has reached a major crossroad with respect to its mission, and the future of the juvenile court is in question. But to discuss juvenile justice without considering the larger economic, social, and cultural context would be foolish. We can only skim the surface of current trends, but even a cursory glance at the present and the immediate future suggests that there are important issues that must be included when considering the kind of juvenile justice system the United States needs.

The juvenile justice system was founded during a time of social disorder that has been linked to the Industrial Revolution, when new industries were forming, agricultural societies were being converted into urban industrial societies, urban areas were rapidly growing in size, and immigration was introducing new languages and cultures into already disorganized environments (Empey 1978). This period of social disruption and that of the 1960s dramatically affected both the nature of the adolescent experience and America's construction of juvenile justice. In the first instance, new systems of social control were formed to manage relationships between children and adolescents and the larger community. Child labor laws, mandatory education, and the juvenile court reduced the options of young people in keeping with the needs and values of those groups that were shaping the future of this new nation. The 1960s brought about a redefinition of the power of children and adolescents with regard to systems of authority. Young people were granted new rights and a greater role in shaping their own futures, creating uncertainty and tension about the proper role of adult authority.

During 1998, the population of the United States grew by more than 2.3 million, and in the year 2000, it was 12 million larger than in 1995, when the total population was estimated to have stood at 263 million (Day 1996a). By 2010, another 25 million Americans will be added, and by 2050, the U.S. population is projected to be 50 percent larger than in 1995. Surprisingly, these changes are occurring in the midst of a slowdown in U.S. population growth.

The U.S. population is also aging. That is, growth is greatest among persons in their 50s, whose numbers are expected to double between 1996 and 2006, and the group 85 and older, which will double in size by 2025 (Day 1996a). By the year 2030, the 65-and-over segment of the population will grow to 20 percent of the population, up from its current level of 13 percent. The 15-to-20 age group, which began growing in 1991 after a lull, will peak in 2010, as will the 45-to-50 age group (Day 1996a). Adolescents ages 15 to 20 will reach 21.7 million in 2010, up from 17.7 million in 1990. Coincidentally, as this adolescent bulge hits its peak, the children of the previous baby boom will begin retiring. In the long run, even though the numbers of children under 18 will continue to grow, young people will not comprise a greater portion of the population than they have in the recent past (Day 1996a; Poe-Yamagata 1998).

Racial and ethnic diversity will continue to challenge our society. Of the more than 2.3-million increase in the population from 1997 to 1998, 900,000 were Hispanic and 459,000 were African-American (Day 1996a). The non-Hispanic white population is projected to drop proportionately from its current level of 72 percent to only 53 percent by 2050, and the number of African-Americans will double by 2050, but the segment of the population that will grow most rapidly is the Hispanic-origin population. Hispanics will add the largest number of persons to the U.S. population every year for the next half century and are likely to be the second largest race/ethnic group by 2010.

For young people these changes are especially significant when we consider the combined age and racial/ethnic changes taking place. While the population of the United States is aging, non-Hispanic whites will comprise a much larger proportion of the over-65 age group than the under-18 age group (Day 1996a). Due to differences in fertility rates and high levels of Hispanic immigration, by 2030, non-Hispanic whites will comprise less than half of the under-18 age group but three-fourths of senior citizens. In 1996, the median age among

At the close of the 20th century, the juvenile system appears to be having increasing difficulty dealing with its inherently contradictory missions of adolescent control and adolescent welfare. The antithetical dimensions are captured in the dilemma that "the child is a criminal and the criminal is a child."

white non-Hispanics was 36.9 in contrast to the median age for Hispanics (26.4) and black non-Hispanics (29.5). By the year 2010, the median age for whites is projected to be 41.0, while for Hispanics the median age will grow to only 27.7 and for black non-Hispanics will reach 30.9. Given America's history of race relations and the impact of resource concerns on racial conflict (Beck and Tolnay 1995; Kennedy 1997), the interaction of age and race/ethnicity promises to be a volatile part of the political equation of the 21st century.

Median incomes in the United States have been rising sharply since 1991 (U.S. Bureau of the Census 1998). Except for significant dips in the 1970s and early 1990s, the overall economic picture is positive. The median income of U.S. workers has grown 58.3 percent since 1947, and real per capita income has grown by 78.6 percent since 1967. This growth is not evenly distributed, however. The incomes of African-Americans and Hispanics are far below those of whites, Asians, and Pacific Islanders. Since 1975, all racial and ethnic groups, except for Hispanics, have experienced income increases. Incomes of Hispanics have remained unchanged and since 1993 have fallen below those of African-Americans.

With respect to Hispanics, the most rapidly growing racial and ethnic segment in our society, income disparity is increasing (U.S. Bureau of the Census 1998). In 1997, the per capita income of Hispanics was half that of whites. Income for blacks is increasing but at a rate slower than that for whites, and African-American per capita income is barely larger than that for Hispanics. With income disparity increasing during a time of prosperity, economic pressures on urban racial and ethnic minorities will undoubtedly grow.

While the number of youths living in poverty has increased over the past two decades (U.S. Bureau of the Census 1999b), this picture varies across racial and ethnic groups. Overall, the increase in the number of youths living in poverty over the past 2 years has been 42 percent, but for Hispanic youths this increase has been 116 percent. For white families with children under 18, the percent living in poverty is increasing (U.S. Bureau of the Census 1999b). In 1977, the percentage in poverty figure for white families was 9.6; it had increased to 13.0 percent by 1997. For black families with children, there has been some fluctuation in percentage in poverty, from 34.2 percent in 1977 to 36.6 percent in 1987 and down to 30.5 percent in 1997, but the figures are consistently large. Among families of Hispanic origin, the recent figures are similar to those of blacks: 25.3 percent in 1977, 31.9 percent in 1987, and 30.4 percent in 1997. Given these economic trends, the proportion of families in each racial group that live in poverty is not likely to decline.

A terminal condition?

At the close of the 20th century, the juvenile system appears to be having increasing difficulty dealing with its inherently contradictory missions of adolescent control and adolescent welfare. The antithetical dimensions are captured in the dilemma that "the child is a criminal and the criminal is a child" (Feld 1993a). The system's reputation for inconsistency and arbitrariness continues to plague it. A participant observer of the Nation's largest juvenile justice system, Los Angeles, has captured the essential realities of the system today: "That is the heartbreak of the Juvenile Court, the wonder of it, and the scandal. Heartbreak, because every kid cannot be saved. Wonder, that this broken, battered, outgunned system saves even one child. Scandal, because it so seldom tries to do anything at all" (Humes 1996, 371).

Any of three general scenarios seem possible for the future of the juvenile system: (1) abolition, with functions merged into the adult criminal system; (2) adaptation, largely by continuing to jettison to the criminal system those youths who are popularly considered unsalvageable while developing new modalities for dealing with those deemed reformable; or (3) expansion, with the court's traditional welfare rationale embracing at least some varieties of adult criminality.

Calls for abolition of the juvenile court comport with contemporary public sentiment that focuses on the depravity of youths who commit crimes, particularly violent crimes. For example, Feld, Rosenberg, and Bazemore (1993) argue that the court's founding rationale regarding the provision of social services in a judicial setting is inherently inconsistent. Judicial mechanisms focus fundamentally on punishment and (what may be the same thing) coercive rehabilitation. They do not address larger social issues (e.g., family, housing, education, and health) that are the crux of the needs of youths who find themselves captured by the juvenile system. The adult criminal court purportedly would do as much to benefit adolescents who commit crimes as the juvenile court does. To compensate for diminished responsibility of youths vis-a-vis adults, a "youth discount" might be applied in sentencing (Feld, Rosenberg, and Bazemore 1993).

Critics of this approach (e.g., Rosenberg 1993) note that the procedural guarantees of adult criminal courts are elusive for most adult criminal defendants. If plea bargaining becomes anywhere near as ubiquitous for youthful defendants as it is for adult defendants, then deficiencies in procedural due process are merely spread over a larger population of criminal court defendants.

Especially since the mid-20th century, the juvenile court has exhibited a remarkable ability to endure through adaptation; it has been termed "an institutional chameleon" (Schwartz, Weiner, and Enosh 1998, 548):

> [T]he juvenile court has been almost uniquely positioned among justice system agencies to be able to intone, without blanching, whatever bromide suits the moment. It has been able to do so because its mission and mandate have been so broad as to be indefinite, thereby permitting an almost limitless set of messages to be crafted that reasonably fall within its purview.

In juxtaposition to the original intent of the formulators of the juvenile system as one into which youths should be diverted, the recent focus has been on diverting youths out of established, formal systems. It has been noted that "the contemporary juvenile court has become just another agency within a complex system of juvenile justice" (Singer 1998, 510). The most prevalent, though risky, technique of adaptation has been the court's tendency to slough off controversial classes of cases. At the lower end, "status offense" jurisdiction has been channeled to less formal mechanisms as the court has focused on more serious matters. More significantly, at the other end of the spectrum, since the late 1960s, the court has relinquished power over increasing numbers of cases to the adult criminal courts. Though ostensibly such transfers are grounded in a youth's maturity and personal moral culpability, they tend frequently to represent frustration with youths who are not transformed into law-abiding citizens through the strained resources of the juvenile system (Federle 1996).

Prosecuting youths in adult criminal courts normally entails the legal process known as the "waiver." In a move that betrays the hollowness of its theoretical philosophical foundations (viz., *parens patriae*), the juvenile court officially washes its hands of youths, delivering them over to punishment by the "adult" system. More recently, the trend has been for legislatures to simplify this task by codifying certain crimes as completely outside the jurisdiction of the juvenile court or to vest with the prosecution the awesome discretion of deciding whether a case should be brought into adult or juvenile court. Issues of so-called reverse waiver arise when youths seek to have their cases returned to juvenile court.

The popularity of defining youths as adult criminals is evidenced by the array of mechanisms that exist to get or keep youths in criminal court. A recent analysis of State transfer provisions noted that discretionary waiver exists in 46 States, statutory exclusion in 28 States, "once an adult, always an adult" clauses in 31 States, direct file by the prosecution in 15 States, "rebuttable presumption" waiver in 15 States, and mandatory waiver in 14 States (Griffin, Torbet, and Szymanski 1998). Reverse waiver provisions exist in 23 States.

A substantial body of research has accumulated on waiver processes. Generally, studies fail to find a coherent legal rationale underlying waiver processes in any particular court. For example, for youths who have not previously been "waived" to criminal court, severity of the present crime did not distinguish those who are waived from those who remain in juvenile court (Lee 1994). In a State where waiver was a prosecutorial decision, most youths who were waived were charged with felonies, but only a small fraction were charged with violent felonies against the person, and nearly one-quarter had no prior criminal record (Bishop, Frazier, and Henretta 1989). Indeed, youths transferred are frequently incorrigible property offenders (Poulos and Orchowsky 1994). Additionally, both race/ethnicity and gender have been associated statistically with prosecutorial requests for transfer (Dawson 1992).

Ironically, unless the crime at issue is a patently serious one, youthful offenses may be taken less seriously by adult courts than by juvenile courts. For youths involved in crimes against the person, punishment is generally dispensed more liberally in adult than in juvenile court, but youths involved in property crimes (including those with an extensive history of such crimes) appear to receive harsher sanctions in juvenile court than in adult court, where the crimes normally handled make the juvenile offenses pale in comparison (Barnes and Franz 1989). Also, one recent study that followed transferred and nontransferred youths for a 2-year period found that a larger proportion of the former committed new offenses, leading the authors to conclude that "[i]f legislatures and courts intend to deter youths from committing additional offenses by subjecting those who persist in delinquency to the more severe punishment of the adult criminal justice system, our data indicate that they are not achieving that goal" (Podkopacz and Feld 1996). Another study used matched cases tracked for a period of 7 years and concluded that transfer was associated with higher frequency of re-arrest, controlling for type of offense (Winner et al. 1997). Also, this same study found that, irrespective of the original offense, transferred youths who were rearrested were apprehended more often and more quickly than were nontransferred youths who were rearrested.

One significant component of system adaptation in the 1990s has been the trend toward restorative responses to adolescent criminality. These models hearken to the early days of the juvenile court in their informality. They are dependent on a sense of community among those affected by the youth's actions, and they seek through mediation and dialogue to repair, insofar as possible, the harm done and to integrate the youth into the local society (Bazemore and Umbreit 1995). Unfortunately, such endeavors have tended somewhat to devolve into simplistic schemes that are adopted superficially by juvenile justice organizations, but that involve no meaningful change within entrenched organizational cultures fossilized in older, incompatible models (Bazemore 1992). Additionally, some purportedly "restorative" models are inherently contradictory in that their latent bases are essentially heavily punitive. For example, the popular, so-called balanced approach purports to balance three objectives: accountability, community protection, and competency development. However, the first two objectives are largely punitive, and only the last is focused on the youth's well-being.

It has been proposed that the historical, individualized, rehabilitative underpinnings of the juvenile court may profitably be used in a variety of adult criminal cases. Though this scenario defies the conventional wisdom of the current era, it does merit consideration. Among its rationales are the following: there appears to be no appreciable difference in severity between adult crimes and juvenile crimes; an adult's criminal behavior is most apt to decline over time, whereas a juvenile's is likely on the ascent until adulthood; limitations on the stigmatic aspects of the criminal process are apt to benefit adults as much as they benefit children; and youths are not necessarily more malleable than adults with regard to treatment (Hirschi and Gottfredson 1993). It has been suggested that a unified system would obviate the fictional, binary opposition that is presupposed by the current dual system, enabling the courts to recognize the gradations in autonomy/dependency and competency/incompetency that exist in the real world for both children and adults: "[f]reed of the requirement that an all-or-nothing determination be made, judges could recognize fine gradations in dependency, malleability, and responsibility as mitigating factors in sentencing" (Ainsworth 1995).

Conclusions

Our view of adolescence has changed from the one that inspired the creators of the juvenile court. Current emphases on accountability and offense-based policies indicate that in today's culture, adolescence is a subset of adulthood rather than childhood. There is a certain instability in this view, however. Ambivalence regarding adolescent autonomy can be seen in the many inconsistencies found in youth policy and case law. And the imagery of delinquency reflects the schizoid nature of juvenile justice: Are delinquents superpredators or naive risk takers? Is it more useful to think of delinquents as risks to public safety or as developing preadults? Should juvenile justice decisionmakers focus on offense behavior or on the developmental needs of their young charges? Should juvenile court legislation emphasize personal accountability for offense behavior or rehabilitation?

America has seen a drop in the rates of every category of serious crime during the 1990s that had been preceded by dramatic increases. LaFree (1998) argues that these changes are causally related to the strength of social institutions that act to manage socialization, provide informal and formal social controls, and protect institutional members. Moore and Tonry (1998), examining trends in youth violence, attribute increases in juvenile violence and victimization between 1985 and 1995 to an increase in size of the juvenile population inter-acting with two parallel trends: increased poverty among families in urban areas and a developing culture of violence. The picture of economic decline and structural disintegration of urban areas and families during the 1970s and 1980s are hypothesized as the context within which gangs, crack cocaine, and guns interacted to produce high levels of conflict that were more lethal than ever before.

The marginalization of minority communities has been fueled by reduced Federal funding to inner cities, urban decay, economic stagnation, and lack of meaningful education and job opportunities (Wilson 1987). Many have expressed concern about the "vicious cycle" perpetuated in inner-city neighbor-hoods by these and other factors. Examination of social indicators reveals a downward spiral in the quality of life for low-income and minority children. Social segregation and isolation may concentrate the negative influence of envi-ronmental factors on inner-city minority communities, resulting in withdrawal and apathy for some and explosive anger for others (Bernard 1990).

Although crime and responses to crime may be related, other forces shape both, and our ability to prepare for juvenile justice in the new millennium will de-pend on the scenarios we develop from our understanding of these relation-ships, the preferred futures we envision, and our capacity to adapt to the unexpected. From our current vantage point, we see a population of U.S. citi-zens that is growing, that is aging, that is becoming more diverse, and that is prospering economically. In spite of cautions regarding the growing number of adolescents in the next decade, proportionately, there is no upward trend for this age group. Instead, it is the senior citizen segment of our population that is growing.

The U.S. population is becoming more diverse. Non-Hispanic whites will make up a smaller proportion of the population, while the greatest increase will be among Hispanics. The Hispanic population will soon likely replace blacks as

> *Perhaps the greatest danger of juvenile justice as we enter a new century has been its clear propensity to further marginalize particular sociodemographic groups.*

the group for which juvenile justice system resources are most concentrated. Hispanics will soon dominate the population of persons under 18, at the same time that their real income levels are dropping and they are, as a group, least involved in our system of education. The patterns of social marginalization and poverty already present within this population appear to be worsening. We are concerned, too, that as demands for government resources increase among the growing senior segment of the population, a group that is dominated by whites and the well educated, the ethnically diverse youth population will lose ground.

In spite of the apparent prosperity currently enjoyed by a large proportion of the U.S. population, poverty, immigration, and racial and ethnic diversity will continue to produce significant social problems. Given this context, the juvenile justice system must attend to the need for community involvement and support of involved parents, openly acknowledge issues of race and ethnicity, and find ways to engage youths in education, particularly those who are members of minority groups.

Facilitating strategic thinking in these areas are advances in delinquency and research. Theory development has benefited greatly from the positivistic approach. In particular, the influence of the Chicago School sociologists was pervasive. At the same time, increased interest in how effective laws, institutions, and justice policies can influence behavior and reduce delinquency is likely to continue. Although delinquency studies in the 20th century have been heavily quantitative, the ethnographic approach has also continued, as evidenced by excellent recent accounts of youth street culture (Anderson 1998), the role of guns in youth violence (Fagan and Wilkinson 1998), juvenile gang membership and structure (Hagedorn 1988; Miller 1998), and juvenile involvement in illegal drug use and sales (Williams 1989). We will continue to see increased interest in interdisciplinary, multilevel, and contextual approaches, as well as more attention to changes in behavior over the life course.

It is interesting to note how significant decreases in juvenile violence in the late 1990s continue to be accompanied by ever-increasing demands to get tough on juvenile crime. Property crimes by juveniles greatly outnumber violent crimes. Juvenile arrests for status offenses have increased dramatically, suggesting an across-the-board, get-tough policy unrelated to actual criminal behavior. We will continue to witness great concern with the problem of school violence, even though very few incidents cause the kind of injury or death that is apparently driving the concern. The changing structure and differentiation of gangs will remain a lead topic, especially as those gangs become more embedded in economic, entrepreneurial contexts. The role of firearms in relation to juvenile violence will probably draw great policy attention in coming years. The superpredator hypothesis has thus far received little support, and more sound projections may hopefully inform public policy as our knowledge and methods improve in the future.

The myth of the violent superpredator is belied even by official statistics. To recapitulate some of the salient points made above, about 4 percent of juvenile arrests are for violent crimes. The vast majority of crimes (especially violent crimes) are committed by adults. Over the past 25 years, a decreasing proportion of both property crime and (more markedly) violent crime has been committed by juveniles. Though juvenile arrests for violent crimes increased in the 1980s and early 1990s, those rates have declined since 1994 even though the juvenile population has increased. Likewise, homicides by juveniles increased significantly from 1988 to 1994, but they have declined since then. At all times, homicides by juveniles have remained a small proportion of all homicides, reaching a high-water mark of only 16 percent of all homicides in 1994. Juvenile involvement in crime remains primarily in those areas in which it has existed throughout the century: property and nonserious crime.

The hypocrisy of the system is that it fails to confront the basic values that underlie the issue of responsibility, particularly social responsibility. Treatment and punishment are often commingled, so that injustice is apt to be the principal perception of those caught up in systems of what we so carelessly term juvenile "justice." Ayers' (1997, 41) insightful comments on the juvenile court are applicable to the entire juvenile system:

> Young people in Juvenile Court are simultaneously pure *and* rotten, immaculate *and* corrupt, angels *and* brutes. We must love and understand the little unformed souls, even as we beat the devil out of the wicked, wayward youth. These seemingly contradictory ideas are united by a single, severe assumption: *We*—the respectable, the prosperous, the superior, and (especially in modern times) the professional—know what is best for *Them*—the masses, the poor, the outcast, the wretched of the earth—in short, our clients. We know what is best for them at all times and in all circumstances and without a doubt . . . . [The objects of our interest] are rendered voiceless and faceless. (emphasis in original)

Perhaps the greatest danger of juvenile justice as we enter a new century has been its clear propensity to further marginalize particular sociodemographic groups. The children of the immigrant rabble of the early 20th century were replaced in the latter part of the century by children of color. As was true of the unpopular, urban, European immigrants at the beginning of the century, high proportions of families who are racial and ethnic minorities live in poverty. We have noted that population projections for the 21st century predict great increases in the proportions of Hispanic citizens. The gross economic disadvantage that exists for minority families—especially Hispanic and African-American—needs to be seen in the new century as a preeminently important challenge for juvenile justice, not as a cultural blight that produces deviants rather than prosocial human beings.

The dawn of the new millennium beckons. Juvenile justice, if it is to be worthy of its name, has the opportunity at the beginning of its second century to reengineer itself toward much greater social good and much less individual harm. Of all fields, juvenile justice is truly one with the ability to shape posterity, for good or for ill.

Notes

1. Of course, excruciatingly detailed qualitative work by early delinquency researchers such as Thrasher was also *empirical*, although the observations were largely qualitative rather than quantitative.

2. See: President's Commission on Law Enforcement and Administration of Justice (1968) and U.S. Department of Justice (1998).

3. The recent Juvenile Justice Action Plan (Coordinating Council on Juvenile Justice and Delinquency Prevention 1996) illustrates an uneasy balance of positivist (e.g., prevention and treatment) as well as classical principles (e.g., individual accountability and sanctions).

4. Space precludes detailed discussion here, but for excellent discussions and examples of the use of HLM (hierarchical linear modeling) to analyze criminological data, see articles by Elliott et al. (1996); Perkins and Taylor (1996); Rountree and Land (1996); Rountree, Land, and Miethe (1994); Sampson, Raudenbush, and Earls (1997); and Welsh, Greene, and Jenkins (1999).

References

Ainsworth, Janet E. 1999. Re-imagining childhood and reconstructing the legal order: The case for abolishing the juvenile court. In *Readings in juvenile justice administration*, edited by Barry Feld. New York: Oxford University Press.

———. 1995. Youth justice in a unified court: Responses to critics of juvenile court abolition. *Boston College Law Review* 36:927–951.

Anderson, David C. 1998. Curriculum, culture, and community: The challenge of school violence. In *Youth violence,* edited by Michael Tonry and Mark H. Moore. Vol. 24 of *Crime and justice: A review of research.* Chicago: University of Chicago Press.

Anderson, Elijah. 1998. The social ecology of youth violence. In *Youth violence,* edited by Michael Tonry and Mark H. Moore. Vol. 24 of *Crime and justice: A review of research.* Chicago: University of Chicago Press.

Andrews, Donald A., Ivan Zinger, Robert D. Hoge, James Bonta, Paul Gendreau, and Francis T. Cullen. 1990. Does correctional treatment work? A clinically relevant and psychologically informed meta-analysis. *Criminology* 28:369–404.

Aries, Philippe. 1962. *Centuries of childhood.* Translated by Robert Bladick. New York: Alfred A. Knopf.

Arrigo, Bruce A., and Robert C. Schehr. 1998. Restoring justice for juveniles: A critical analysis of victim-offender mediation. *Justice Quarterly* 15 (4): 629–666.

Asquith, Stewart. 1983. *Children and justice: Decision-making in children's hearings and juvenile courts.* Edinburgh: Edinburgh University Press.

Austin, Joe, and Michael Nevin Willard. 1998. Introduction: Angels of history, demons of culture. In *Generations of youth: Youth cultures and history in twentieth-century America,* edited by Joe Austin and Michael Nevin Willard. New York: New York University Press.

Ayers, William. 1997. *A kind and just parent: The children of juvenile court.* Boston: Beacon Press.

Barak, Gregg. 1994. *Media, process, and the social construction of crime.* New York: Garland Publishing.

Barnes, Carole Wolff, and Randal S. Franz. 1989. Questionably adult: Determinants and effects of the juvenile waiver decision. *Justice Quarterly* 6 (1): 117–135.

Bastian, Lisa D., and Bruce M. Taylor. 1991. *School crime.* NCJ 131645. Washington, D.C.: U.S. Department of Justice, Bureau of Justice Statistics.

Bazemore, Gordon. 1992. On mission statements and reform in juvenile justice: The case of the "balanced approach." *Federal Probation* 56 (3): 64–70.

Bazemore, Gordon, and Mark Umbreit. 1995. Rethinking the sanctioning function of juvenile court: Retributive or restorative responses to youth crime. *Crime & Delinquency* 41 (3): 296–316.

Beck, E.M., and Stewart E. Tolnay. 1995. Violence toward African-Americans in the era of the white lynch mob. In *Ethnicity, race, and crime: Perspectives across time and place*, edited by Darnell F. Hawkins. Albany: State University of New York Press.

Bernard, Thomas J. 1992. *The cycle of juvenile justice*. New York: Oxford University Press.

———. 1990. Angry aggression among the "truly disadvantaged." *Criminology* 28 (1): 73–96.

Bernard, Thomas J., and Jeffrey B. Snipes. 1996. Theoretical integration in criminology. In *Crime and justice: A review of research*, edited by Michael Tonry. Vol. 20. Chicago: University of Chicago Press.

Biderman, Albert D., and James P. Lynch. 1991. *Understanding crime incidence statistics: Why the UCR diverges from the NCS*. New York: Springer-Verlag.

Bishop, Donna M., and Charles E. Frazier. 1996. Race effects in juvenile justice decision-making: Findings of a statewide analysis. *Journal of Criminal Law and Criminology* 86 (2): 392–414.

Bishop, Donna M., Charles E. Frazier, and John C. Henretta. 1989. Prosecutorial waiver: Case study of a questionable reform. *Crime & Delinquency* 35 (2): 179–201.

Blumstein, Alfred. 1995. Violence by young people: Why the deadly nexus? *National Institute of Justice Journal*:1–9.

Blumstein, Alfred, Richard Curtis, Jeffrey Fagan, June Kim, Gary LaFree, Robert Nash Parker, Irving Piliavin, Richard Rosenfeld, Christopher Uggen, and Franklin E. Zimring. 1998. Crime's decline—Why? *National Institute of Justice Journal* 237:7–21.

Bourgois, Philippe. 1997. In search of Horatio Alger: Culture and ideology in the crack economy. In *Crack in America: Demon drugs and social justice*, edited by Craig Reinarman and Harry G. Levine. Berkeley: University of California Press.

———. 1995. *In search of respect: Selling crack in el barrio*. Cambridge: Cambridge University Press.

Braithwaite, John. 1989. *Crime, shame, and reintegration*. Cambridge: Cambridge University Press.

Brantingham, Paul J., and Patricia L. Brantingham, eds. 1991. *Environmental criminology*. Prospect Heights, Illinois: Waveland Press.

Brantingham, Paul J., and C. Ray Jeffery. 1991. Afterword: Crime, space, and criminological theory. In *Environmental criminology*, edited by P.J. Brantingham and P.L. Brantingham. Prospect Heights, Illinois: Waveland Press.

Brendtro, L.K., and N.J. Long. 1994. Violence begets violence: Breaking conflict cycles. *Journal of Emotional and Behavioral Problems: Reclaiming Children and Youth* 3:2–7.

Brooks-Gunn, Jean, Greg J. Duncan, Pamela Klato Klebanov, and Naomi Sealand. 1993. Do neighborhoods influence child and adolescent development? *American Journal of Sociology* 99:353–395.

Browning, Katherine, and Rolf Loeber. 1999. *Highlights of findings from the Pittsburgh youth study*. OJJDP Fact Sheet 95, FS–9995. Washington, D.C.: U.S. Department of Justice, Office of Juvenile Justice and Delinquency Prevention.

Burgess, Ernest W. [1925] 1967. The growth of the city: An introduction to a research project. In *The city*, edited by Robert E. Park, Ernest W. Burgess, and Roderick D. McKenzie. Chicago: University of Chicago Press.

Bursik, Robert J., Jr. 1988. Social disorganization and theories of crime and delinquency: Problems and prospects. *Criminology* 26:519–552.

Bursik, Robert J., Jr., and Harold Grasmick. 1993. *Neighborhoods and crime: The dimensions of effective community control*. New York: Lexington Books.

Butts, Jeffrey, and A.V. Harrell. 1998. *Delinquents or criminals: Policy options for young offenders*. Washington, D.C.: Urban Institute.

Catalano, R.F., and J.D. Hawkins. 1996. The social development model: A theory of antisocial behavior. In *Delinquency and crime: Current theories*, edited by J.D. Hawkins. New York: Cambridge University Press.

Chandler, Kathryn A., Christopher D. Chapman, Michael R. Rand, and Bruce M. Taylor. 1998. *Students' reports of school crime: 1989 and 1995*, NCES 98–241/NCJ 169607. Washington, D.C.: U.S. Departments of Education and Justice.

Chesney-Lind, Meda, and Randall G. Shelden. 1992. *Girls: Delinquency and juvenile justice*. Pacific Grove, California: Brooks/Cole Publishing Company.

Cloward, Richard, and Lloyd Ohlin. 1960. *Delinquency and opportunity*. New York: Free Press.

Cohen, Albert K. 1955. *Delinquent boys*. New York: Free Press.

Cole, George F., and Christopher E. Smith. 1998. *The American system of criminal justice*. 8th ed. Belmont, California: Wadsworth Publishing Company.

Cook, Philip J., and John H. Laub. 1998. The unprecedented epidemic in youth violence. In *Youth violence*, edited by Michael Tonry and Mark H. Moore. Vol. 24 of *Crime and justice: A review of research*. Chicago: University of Chicago Press.

Coordinating Council on Juvenile Justice and Delinquency Prevention. 1996. *Combating violence and delinquency: The National Juvenile Justice Action Plan*. NCJ 157106. Washington, D.C.: U.S. Department of Justice, Office of Juvenile Justice and Delinquency Prevention.

Corley, Charles J., Timothy S. Bynum, and Madeline Wordes. 1995. Conceptions of family and juvenile court processes: A qualitative assessment. *Justice System Journal* 18 (2): 157–172.

Curry, G. David, Robert A. Ball, and Scott H. Decker. 1996. Estimating the national scope of gang crime from law enforcement data. In *Gangs in America*, edited by C. Ronald Huff. Newbury Park, California: Sage Publications.

Curtis, Richard. 1998. The improbable transformation of inner-city neighborhoods: Crime, violence, drugs, and youths in the 1990s. *National Institute of Justice Journal* 237 (October): 16–17.

Dawson, Robert O. 1992. An empirical study of Kent style juvenile transfers to criminal court. *St. Mary's Law Journal* 23:975–1053.

Day, J.C. 1996a. *Population projections of the United States by age, sex, race, and Hispanic origin: 1995 to 2050.* Current Population Reports. Washington, D.C.: U.S. Bureau of the Census.

———. 1996b. *Projections of the number of households and families in the United States: 1995–2110.* Current Population Reports. Washington, D.C.: U.S. Bureau of the Census.

DiIulio, John J., Jr. 1997. Law enforcement can effectively combat crime. In *Juvenile crime: Opposing viewpoints*, edited by A.E. Sadler. San Diego: Greenhaven Press.

———. 1996. They're coming: Florida's youth crime bomb. *Impact* (Spring): 25–27.

Duster, Troy. 1987. Crime, youth, and unemployment and the black underclass. *Journal of Research in Crime and Delinquency* 33:300–316.

Elder, G. 1985. Perspectives on the life course. In *Life course dynamics*, edited by G. Elder. Ithaca, New York: Cornell University Press.

Elliott, Delbert S. 1994. Serious violent offenders: Onset, developmental course, and termination—The American Society of Criminology 1993 Presidential address. *Criminology* 32:1–21.

Elliott, Delbert S., David Huizinga, and Suzanne S. Ageton. 1985. *Explaining delinquency and drug use*, Newbury Park, California: Sage Publications.

Elliott, Delbert S., David Huizinga, and Scott Menard. 1989. *Multiple problem youth: Delinquency, substance use, and mental health problems.* New York: Springer-Verlag.

Elliott, Delbert S., William Julius Wilson, David Huizinga, Robert J. Sampson, Amanda Elliott, and Bruce Rankin. 1996. The effects of neighborhood disadvantage on adolescent development. *Journal of Research in Crime and Delinquency* 33:389–426.

Empey, LaMar. 1982. *American delinquency: Its meaning and construction.* 2d ed. Homewood, Illinois: Dorsey Press.

———. 1978. *American delinquency: Its meaning and construction.* Homewood, Illinois: Dorsey Press.

Empey, LaMar T., and Mark Stafford. 1991. *American delinquency: Its meaning and construction.* Belmont, California: Wadsworth Publishing Company.

Fagan, Jeffrey. 1996. Gangs, drugs, and neighborhood change. In *Gangs in America,* edited by C. Ronald Huff. 2d ed. Thousand Oaks, California: Sage Publications.

Fagan, Jeffrey, Ellen Slaughter, and Eliot Hartstone. 1987. Blind justice? The impact of race on the juvenile process. *Crime & Delinquency* 33 (2): 224–258.

Fagan, Jeffrey, and Deanna L. Wilkinson. 1998. Guns, youth violence, and social identity in inner cities. In *Youth violence,* edited by Michael Tonry and Mark H. Moore. Vol. 24 of *Crime and justice: A review of research.* Chicago: University of Chicago Press.

Farrington, David P. 1998. Predictors, causes, and correlates of male youth violence. In *Youth violence,* edited by Michael Tonry and Mark H. Moore. Vol. 24 of *Crime and justice: A review of research.* Chicago: University of Chicago Press.

———. 1986. Age and crime. In *Crime and justice: An annual review of research,* edited by Michael Tonry and Norval Morris. Vol. 7. Chicago: University of Chicago Press.

———. 1973. Self-reports of deviant behavior: Predictive and stable? *Journal of Criminal Law and Criminology* 64:99–110.

Farrington, David P., Rolf Loeber, Magda Stouthamer-Loeber, Welmoet B. Van Kammen, and Laura Schmidt. 1996. Self-reported delinquency and a combined delinquency seriousness scale based on boys, mothers, and teachers: Concurrent and predictive validity for African-Americans and Caucasians. *Criminology* 34:493–517.

Federle, Katherine Hunt. 1996. Emancipation and execution: Transferring children to criminal court in capital cases. *Wisconsin Law Review* 3:447–494.

Feld, Barry C. 1993a. Criminalizing the American juvenile court. In *Crime and justice: A review of research,* edited by Michael Tonry. Vol. 17. Chicago: University of Chicago Press.

———. 1993b. *Justice for children: The right to counsel and the juvenile court.* Boston: Northeastern University Press.

———. 1991. Justice by geography: Urban, suburban, and rural variations in juvenile administration. *Journal of Criminal Law and Criminology* 82 (1): 156–210.

———. 1989. The right to counsel in juvenile court: An empirical study of when lawyers appear and the difference they make. *Journal of Criminal Law and Criminology* 79:1185–1346.

———. 1988. Juvenile court meets the principle of offense: Punishment, treatment, and the difference it makes. *Boston University Law Review* 68 (5): 821–915.

Feld, Barry C., I.M. Rosenberg, and Gordon Bazemore. 1993. *The juvenile court: Dynamic, dysfunctional, or dead?* Philadelphia: Center for the Study of Youth Policy, University of Pennsylvania.

Ferraro, Kenneth F. 1994. *Fear of crime: Interpreting victimization risk.* Albany: State University of New York Press.

Ferraro, Kenneth F., and Randy L. LaGrange. 1987. The measurement of fear of crime. *Sociological Inquiry* 57:70–101.

Finestone, Harold. 1977. *Victims of change: Juvenile delinquency in American society.* Westport, Connecticut: Greenwood Press.

———. 1976. The delinquent and society: The Shaw and McKay tradition. In *Delinquency, crime, and society*, edited by James F. Short. Chicago: University of Chicago Press.

Fox, James A. 1996. *Trends in juvenile violence: A report to the United States Attorney General on current and future rates of juvenile offending.* Boston: Northeastern University Press.

Fox, Sanford J. 1970. Juvenile justice reform: An historical perspective. *Stanford Law Review* 22:1187–1239.

Gardner, Martin R. 1995. Punitive juvenile justice: Some observations on a recent trend. In *The new juvenile justice*, edited by Martin L. Forst. Chicago: Nelson-Hall.

Gibbons, Donald C. 1979. *The criminological enterprise: Theories and perspectives.* Englewood Cliffs, New Jersey: Prentice Hall.

Glueck, Sheldon, and Eleanor Glueck. 1950. *Unraveling juvenile delinquency.* Cambridge: Harvard University Press.

Gottfredson, Gary D. 1984. *The effective school battery.* Odessa, Florida: Psychological Assessment Resources, Inc.

Gottfredson, Gary D., and Denise C. Gottfredson. 1985. *Victimization in schools.* New York: Plenum Press.

Gottfredson, Michael R., and Travis Hirschi. 1990. *A general theory of crime.* Stanford, California: Stanford University Press.

———. 1987. The positive tradition. In *Positive criminology*, edited by Michael R. Gottfredson and Travis Hirschi. Newbury Park, California: Sage Publications.

Gottschalk, Rand, William S. Davidson, Jeffrey P. Meyer, and Leah K. Gensheimer. 1987. Behavioral approaches with juvenile offenders: A meta-analysis of long-term treatment efficacy. In *Behavioral approaches to crime and delinquency*, edited by E.K. Morris and C.J. Braukmann. New York: Plenum Press.

Gove, Walter R., Michael Hughes, and Michael Geerken. 1985. Are Uniform Crime Reports a valid indicator of the index crimes? An affirmative answer with minor qualifications. *Criminology* 23:451–500.

Greenbaum, Stuart. 1997. Kids and guns: From playgrounds to battlegrounds. *Juvenile justice, Journal of the Office of Juvenile Justice and Delinquency Prevention* 3 (2): 3–10.

Greenwood, Peter W. 1992. Substance abuse problems among high-risk youth and potential interventions. *Crime & Delinquency* 38:444–458.

Griffin, Patrick, Patricia Torbet, and Linda Szymanski. 1998. *Trying juveniles as adults in criminal court: An analysis of state transfer provisions*. Report, NCJ 172836. Washington, D.C.: U.S. Department of Justice, Office of Juvenile Justice and Delinquency Prevention.

Hagan, John. 1989. *Structural criminology*. New Brunswick, New Jersey: Rutgers University Press.

Hagedorn, John M. 1994. Neighborhoods, markets, and gang drug organization. *Journal of Research in Crime and Delinquency* 31:264–294.

———. 1991. Gangs, neighborhoods, and public policy. *Social problems* 38:529–542.

———. 1988. *People and folks: Gangs, crime, and the underclass in a Rustbelt city*. Chicago: Lake View Press.

Haller, Mark H. [1963] 1984. *Eugenics: Hereditarian attitudes in American thought*. New Brunswick, New Jersey: Rutgers University Press.

Hanna, J.L. 1988. *Disruptive school behavior: Class, race, and culture*. New York: Holmes and Meier.

Hawkins, J.D., and R.F. Catalano. 1995. *Risk-focused prevention: Using the social development strategy*. Seattle: Developmental Research and Programs.

———. 1992. *Communities that care: Action for drug abuse prevention*. San Francisco: Jossey-Bass.

Hindelang, Michael J. 1973. Causes of delinquency: A partial replication and extension. *Social problems* 20:471–487.

Hindelang, Michael J., Travis Hirschi, and Joseph G. Weis. 1981. *Measuring delinquency.* Beverly Hills: Sage Publications.

Hirschi, Travis. 1969. *Causes of delinquency.* Berkeley: University of California Press.

Hirschi, Travis, and Michael Gottfredson. 1993. Rethinking the juvenile justice system. *Crime & Delinquency* 39 (2): 262–271.

———. 1983. Age and the explanation of crime. *American Journal of Sociology* 89:522–584.

Howell, James C. 1997. *Juvenile justice and youth violence.* Thousand Oaks, California: Sage Publications.

Howell, James C., ed. 1995. *Guide for implementing the comprehensive strategy for serious, violent, and chronic juvenile offenders.* NCJ 153681. Washington, D.C.: U.S. Department of Justice, Office of Juvenile Justice and Delinquency Prevention.

Huizinga, David, and Delbert S. Elliott. 1986. Reassessing the reliability and validity of self-report delinquency measures. *Journal of Quantitative Criminology* 2:293–327.

Humes, Edward. 1996. *No matter how loud I shout: A year in the life of juvenile court.* New York: Simon & Schuster.

Investor's Business Daily. 1999. A generation of workers. 30 April.

Kappeler, Victor E., Mark Blumberg, and Gary W. Potter. 1996. *The mythology of crime and criminal justice.* 2d ed. Prospect Heights, Illinois: Waveland Press.

Kazdin, A.E. 1987. *Conduct disorders in childhood and adolescence.* Newbury Park, California: Sage Publications.

Kelley, Barbara T., David Huizinga, Terence P. Thornberry, and Rolf Loeber. 1997. *Epidemiology of serious violence.* Research Report, NCJ 165152. Washington, D.C.: U.S. Department of Justice, Office of Juvenile Justice and Delinquency Prevention.

Kennedy, David M. 1997. *Juvenile gun violence and gun markets in Boston.* Research Preview, FS 000160. Washington, D.C.: U.S. Department of Justice, National Institute of Justice.

Kennedy, Randall. 1997. *Race, crime, and the law.* New York: Random House.

Klein, Malcolm W. 1995. *The American street gang.* New York: Oxford University Press.

Krisberg, Barry, and James Austin. 1993. *Reinventing juvenile justice*. Newbury Park, California: Sage Publications.

LaFree, Gary. 1998. *Losing legitimacy: Street crime and the decline of social institutions in America*. Boulder, Colorado: Westview Press.

LaGrange, Randy L., and Kenneth F. Ferraro. 1989. Assessing age and gender differences in perceived risk and fear of crime. *Criminology* 27:697–719.

Lawrence, Richard A. 1998. *School crime and juvenile justice*. New York: Oxford University Press.

LeBlanc, Marc, and Rolf Loeber. 1998. Developmental criminology updated. In *Crime and justice: A review of research*, edited by Michael Tonry. Vol. 23. Chicago: University of Chicago Press.

Lee, Leona. 1994. Factors determining waiver in a juvenile court. *Journal of Criminal Justice* 22 (4): 329–339.

Loeber, Rolf, and David P. Farrington, eds. 1998. *Serious and violent juvenile offenders: Risk factors and successful interventions*. Thousand Oaks, California: Sage Publications.

Maguire, Kathleen, and Ann L. Pastore. 1999. Section 4: Introduction, and Table 4.7: Arrests by offense charged and age, United States, 1997. *Sourcebook of criminal justice statistics online*. Retrieved 3 January 2000 from the World Wide Web: http://www.albany.edu/free-tops/docs.sourcebook/1995/about.html.

———. 1997. *Sourcebook of criminal justice statistics—1996*. Washington, D.C.: U.S. Department of Justice, Bureau of Justice Statistics.

Matza, David. 1964. *Delinquency and drift*. New York: John Wiley & Sons.

Matza, David, and Gresham M. Sykes. 1961. Juvenile delinquency and subterranean values. *American Sociological Review* 26:712–719.

McCarthy, Belinda R., and Brent L. Smith. 1986. The conceptualization of discrimination in the juvenile justice process: The impact of administrative factors and screening decisions in juvenile court dispositions. *Criminology* 24 (1): 41–64.

McKenzie, Roderick D. 1925. The ecological approach to the study of the human community. In *The city*, edited by R.E. Park, E.W. Burgess, and R.D. McKenzie. Chicago: University of Chicago Press.

Mennel, Richard. 1973. *Thorns and thistles*. Hanover, New Hampshire: University Press of New England.

Messner, Steven F., and Richard Rosenfeld. 1997. *Crime and the American dream*. 2d ed. Belmont, California: Wadsworth Publishing Company.

Miller, Jerome G. 1991. *Last one over the wall: The Massachusetts experiment in closing reform schools*. Columbus: Ohio State University Press.

Miller, Jody. 1998. Gender and victimization risk among young women in gangs. *Journal of Research in Crime and Delinquency* 35:429–453.

Moore, Mark H. 1995. Public health and criminal justice approaches to prevention. In *Crime and justice: A review of research*, edited by Michael Tonry. Vol. 19. Chicago: University of Chicago Press.

———. 1987. *From children to citizens, volume I: The mandate for juvenile justice*. New York: Springer-Verlag.

Moore, Mark H., and Michael Tonry. 1998. Youth violence in America. In *Youth violence*, edited by Michael Tonry and Mark H. Moore. Vol. 24 of *Crime and justice: A review of research*. Chicago: University of Chicago Press.

Morgan, Gareth. 1997. *Images of organization*. 2d ed. Thousand Oaks, California: Sage Publications.

National School Boards Association. 1993. *Violence in the schools: How America's school boards are safeguarding our children*. Alexandria, Virginia: National School Boards Association.

Park, Robert E., Ernest W. Burgess, and Roderick D. McKenzie, eds. [1925] 1967. *The city*. Chicago: University of Chicago Press.

Perkins, Douglas D., and Ralph B. Taylor. 1996. Ecological assessments of community disorder: Their relationship to fear of crime and theoretical implications. *American Journal of Community Psychology* 24:63–107.

Platt, Anthony M. 1977. *The child savers: The invention of delinquency*. 2d ed. enlarged. Chicago: University of Chicago Press.

Podkopacz, Marcy Rasmussen, and Barry C. Feld. 1996. The end of the line: An empirical study of judicial waiver. *Journal of Criminal Law and Criminology* 82 (2): 449–492.

Poe-Yamagata, Eileen. 1998. The number of youth under age 18 and their proportion of the population, 1950–2020. Adapted from Federal Interagency Forum on Child and Family Statistics. *America's children: Indicators of well-being, 1998* [HTML File]. Washington, D.C. Retrieved 10 December 1998 from the *Office of Juvenile Justice and Delinquency Prevention Statistical Briefing Book* from the World Wide Web: http://ojjdp.ncjrs.org/ojstatbb/qa071.html.

Poulos, Tammy Meredith, and Stan Orchowsky. 1994. Serious juvenile offenders: Predicting the probability of transfer to juvenile court. *Crime & Delinquency* 40 (1): 3–17.

President's Commission on Law Enforcement and Administration of Justice. 1968. *The challenge of crime in a free society*. New York: Avon Books.

Quinney, Richard. 1970. *The social reality of crime*. Boston: Little, Brown and Company.

Reiss, Albert J., Jr., and Jeffrey A. Roth, eds. 1993. *Understanding and preventing violence*. Vol. 1. Washington, D.C.: National Academy Press.

Rosenberg, I.M. 1993. Leaving bad enough alone: A response to the juvenile court abolitionists. *Wisconsin Law Review* 1:163–185.

Roth, Jeffrey. 1994. *Understanding and preventing violence*. Research in Brief, NCJ 145645. Washington, D.C.: U.S. Department of Justice, National Institute of Justice.

Rothman, David. 1980. *Conscience and convenience: The asylum and its alternatives in progressive America*. Boston: Little, Brown and Company.

Rountree, Pamela Wilcox, and Kenneth C. Land. 1996. Perceived risk versus fear of crime: Empirical evidence of conceptually distinct reactions in survey data. *Social Forces* 74:1353–1376.

Rountree, Pamela Wilcox, Kenneth C. Land, and Terance D. Miethe. 1994. Macro-micro integration in the study of victimization: A hierarchical logistic model analysis across Seattle neighborhoods. *Criminology* 32:387–414.

Sampson, Robert J., and Janet L. Lauritsen. 1993. Violent victimization and offending: Individual-, situational-, and community-level risk factors. In *Understanding and Preventing Violence: Social Influences*, edited by Albert J. Reiss, Jr., and Jeffrey A. Roth. Vol. 3. Washington, D.C.: National Academy Press.

Sampson, Robert J., Stephen W. Raudenbush, and Felton Earls. 1997. Neighborhoods and violent crime: A multilevel study of collective efficacy. *Science* 277:918–924.

Schlossman, S., and M. Sedlak. 1983. The Chicago area project. *Crime & Delinquency* 29:398–462.

Schwartz, Ira M., Neil Alan Weiner, and Guy Enosh. 1998. Nine lives and then some: Why the juvenile court does not roll over and die. *Wake Forest Law Review* 33:533–552.

Shaw, Clifford R., and Henry D. McKay. 1942. *Juvenile delinquency and urban areas*. Chicago: University of Chicago Press.

Sheley, Joseph F., Zina T. McGee, and James W. Wright. 1995. *Weapon-related victimization in selected inner-city high school samples*. NCJ 151526. Washington, D.C.: U.S. Department of Justice, National Institute of Justice.

Sheley, Joseph F., and James D. Wright. 1993. *Gun acquisition and possession in selected juvenile samples.* Research Report, NCJ 145326. Washington, D.C.: U.S. Department of Justice, National Institute of Justice.

Short, James F., Jr. 1998. The level of explanation problem revisited—The American Society of Criminology 1997 Presidential address. *Criminology* 36:3–36.

Short, James F., Jr., and F. Ivan Nye. 1958. Extent of unrecorded juvenile delinquency: Tentative conclusions. *Journal of Criminal Law and Criminology* 49:296–302.

Sickmund, Melissa. 1997. Percent change in the public custody facility population, 1983–1995. Adapted from M. Sickmund, H. Snyder, and E. Poe-Yamagata. *Juvenile offenders and victims: 1997 update on violence, OJJDP Statistical Briefing Book.* [HTML File] or [Adobe Acrobat File]. Washington, D.C.: U.S. Department of Justice, Office of Juvenile Justice and Delinquency Prevention. Retrieved 10 December 1999 from the World Wide Web: http://ojjdp.ncjrs.org/ojstatbb/qa057.html.

Singer, Simon I. 1998. Criminal and teen courts as loosely coupled systems of juvenile justice. *Wake Forest Law Review* 33 (3): 509–532.

————. 1996. *Recriminalizing delinquency: Violent juvenile crime and juvenile justice reform.* New York: Cambridge University Press.

Skovron, Sandra Evans, Joseph E. Scott, and Francis T. Cullen. 1995. The death penalty for juveniles: An assessment of public support. In *The new juvenile justice*, edited by Martin L. Forst. Chicago: Nelson-Hall.

Smith, Kristin E., and Amara Bachu. 1999. Women's labor force attachment patterns and maternity leave: A review of the literature. *Population Division Working Paper No. 32.* Washington, D.C.: U.S. Bureau of the Census, Population Division. Retrieved 3 January 2000 from the World Wide Web: http://www.census.gov/population/www/documentation/twps0032/twps0032.html#Labor Force Participation Pre-FMLA.

Snyder, Howard N. 1999. Violent juvenile crime: The number of violent juvenile offenders declines. *Corrections Today* (April): 96–100.

————. 1998. *Juvenile arrests 1997.* Juvenile Justice Bulletin, NCJ 173938. Washington, D.C.: U.S. Department of Justice, Office of Juvenile Justice and Delinquency Prevention.

Snyder, Howard N., and Melissa Sickmund. 1995. *Juvenile offenders and victims: A focus on violence.* Statistics Summary, NCJ 153570. Washington, D.C.: U.S. Department of Justice, Office of Juvenile Justice and Delinquency Prevention.

Snyder, Howard N., Melissa Sickmund, and Eileen Poe-Yamagata. 1996. *Juvenile offenders and victims: 1996 update on violence.* Statistics Summary, NCJ 159107. Washington, D.C.: U.S. Department of Justice, Office of Juvenile Justice and Delinquency Prevention.

Steffensmeier, Darrell, Emilie Anderson Allen, Miles Harer, and Cathy Streifel. 1989. Age and the distribution of crime. *American Sociological Review* 94:803–831.

Sutton, John R. 1985. The juvenile court and social welfare: Dynamics of progressive reform. *Law & Society Review* 19 (1): 107–145.

Sykes, Gresham M., and David Matza. 1957. Techniques of neutralization: A theory of delinquency. *American Journal of Sociology* 22:664–670.

Szymanski, Lynn. 1997. State variations in age restrictions for trying juveniles in criminal court. *NCJJ Snapshot* 2 (2). Pittsburgh: National Center for Juvenile Justice.

Thornberry, Terrence P. 1987. Toward an interactional theory of delinquency. *Criminology* 25:863–887.

Thornberry, Terrence P., ed. 1997. *Developmental theories of crime and delinquency: Advances in theoretical criminology.* Vol. 7. Piscataway, New Jersey: Transaction Publishers.

Thornberry, Terrence P., Melanie Moore, and R.L. Christenson. 1993. The effect of dropping out of high school on subsequent criminal behavior. *Criminology* 23:3–18.

Thrasher, Frederick. 1927. *The gang.* Chicago: University of Chicago Press.

Torbet, Patricia, Richard Gable, Hunter Hurst IV, Imogene Montgomery, Linda Szymanski, and Douglas Thomas. 1996. *State responses to serious and violent juvenile crime.* NCJ 161565. Washington, D.C.: U.S. Department of Justice, Office of Juvenile Justice and Delinquency Prevention.

U.S. Bureau of the Census. 1999a. Historical poverty tables—Families, table 13. Retrieved 3 January 2000 from the World Wide Web: http://www.census.gov/income/histpov/histovpov13.txt.

———. 1999b. Historical poverty tables—Families, table 4. Retrieved 3 January 2000 from the World Wide Web: http://www.census.gov/income/histpov/histovpov4.txt.

———. 1998. Sociodemographic tables—School, tables A1–A5. Retrieved 3 January 2000 from the World Wide Web: http://www.census.gov/prod/3/98pubs/p20-5000.pdf.

U.S. Department of Health and Human Services, Centers for Disease Control and Prevention. 1995. Surveillance summaries: Youth risk behavior surveillance—United States. *Morbidity and Mortality Weekly Report* 44 (No. SS–1). Atlanta.

U.S. Department of Justice, Office of Justice Programs. 1998. *The challenge of crime in a free society: Looking back, looking forward.* Symposium on the 30th Anniversary of the President's Commission on Law Enforcement and Administration of Justice, NCJ 170029. Washington, D.C.

Vold, George B., Thomas J. Bernard, and Jeffrey B. Snipes. 1998. *Theoretical criminology.* 4th ed. New York: Oxford University Press.

Welsh, Wayne N. In press. Teen violence in the U.S.A. In *Teen violence: A global perspective,* edited by Randall Summers and Allan Hoffman. Westport, Connecticut: Greenwood Press.

————. 2000. Effects of school climate on school disorder. *Annals of the American Association of Political and Social Science* 567:88–107.

Welsh, Wayne N., Jack R. Greene, and Patricia H. Jenkins. 1999. School disorder: The influence of individual, institutional, and community factors. *Criminology* 37:73–115.

————. 1998. *Effects of school climate on measures of student fear, victimization, and offending.* Paper presented at the Annual Meeting of the American Society of Criminology, 11 November, Washington, D.C.

Welsh, Wayne N., and Philip W. Harris. 1999. *Criminal justice policy and planning.* Cincinnati: Anderson Publishing Company.

Welsh, Wayne N., Philip W. Harris, and Patricia H. Jenkins. 1996. Reducing overrepresentation of minorities in juvenile justice: Development of community-based programs in Pennsylvania. *Crime & Delinquency* 42 (1): 76–98.

Welsh, Wayne N., Patricia H. Jenkins, and Jack R. Greene. 1999. *Effects of school climate on student misconduct.* Paper presented at the Annual Meeting of the Academy of Criminal Justice Sciences, 10 March, Orlando.

————. 1997. *Building a culture and climate of safety in public schools in Philadelphia: School- based management and violence reduction.* Final Report submitted to the National Institute of Justice and the Center for Public Policy, Temple University, Philadelphia.

Welsh, Wayne N., Patricia H. Jenkins, and Philip W. Harris. 1999. Reducing minority over-representation in juvenile justice: Results of community-based delinquency prevention in Harrisburg. *Journal of Research in Crime and Delinquency* 36:87–110.

Welsh, Wayne N., Robert Stokes, and Jack R. Greene. In press. A macro-level model of school disorder. *Journal of Research in Crime and Delinquency* 37.

Whitaker, C.J., and L.D. Bastian. 1991. *Teenage victims: A national crime survey report.* NCJ 128129. Washington, D.C.: U.S. Department of Justice, Bureau of Justice Statistics.

Whyte, William Foote. 1943. *Street corner society.* Chicago: University of Chicago Press.

Williams, Terry. 1989. *The cocaine kids.* Reading, Massachusetts: Addison-Wesley.

Wilson, John J., and James C. Howell. 1993. *A comprehensive strategy for serious, violent, and chronic juvenile offenders.* Research Report, NCJ 143453. Washington, D.C.: U.S. Department of Justice, Office of Juvenile Justice and Delinquency Prevention.

Wilson, William Julius. 1987. *The truly disadvantaged: The inner city, the underclass, and public policy.* Chicago: University of Chicago Press.

Winner, Lawrence, Lonn Lanza-Kaduce, Donna M. Bishop, and Charles E. Frazier. 1997. The transfer of juveniles to criminal court: Reexamining recidivism over the long term. *Crime & Delinquency* 43 (4): 548–563.

Wizner, Stephen. 1995. On youth crime and the juvenile court. *Boston College Law Review* 36:1025–1035.

Zimring, Franklin E., and Gordon Hawkins. 1998. *Youth violence.* New York: Oxford University Press.

www.ingramcontent.com/pod-product-compliance
Lightning Source LLC
Chambersburg PA
CBHW060002300526
45794CB00003B/1043